A Child
Is Born

Four months old and the center of the world. Sitting on Daddy's knee, he looks around with intense curiosity. The very image of his father, says Grandfather. But with his mother's eyes, says Grandmother. A little more than a year ago he didn't exist at all.

PHOTOGRAPHS

Lennart Nilsson

TEXT

Axel Ingelman-Sundberg

Claes Wirsén

A Child
Is Born

The Drama of Life before Birth in
Unprecedented Photographs

A Practical Guide for the Expectant Mother

A Merloyd Lawrence Book
A Dell Trade Paperback/Seymour Lawrence

A MERLOYD LAWRENCE BOOK
Dell Trade Paperback/Seymour Lawrence Edition
Published by
Dell Publishing Co., Inc.
1 Dag Hammarskjold Plaza
New York, New York 10017

Originally published in Swedish under the title *Ett Barn Blir Till*. Translated by Britt and Claes Wirsen, Annabelle MacMillan.

Copyright © 1965 by Albert Bonniers Forlag, Stockholm

English translation copyright © 1966 by Dell Publishing Co., Inc.

Dell ® TM 681510, Dell Publishing Co., Inc.

ISBN: 0-440-51214-X

Reprinted by arrangement with Delacorte Press/Seymour Lawrence
Printed in the United States of America

Ninth Dell printing—June 1985

Preface

The revolution that occurs in a young woman's body when she becomes pregnant might be compared with another explosion of life force: the rising of sap in the spring. A girl who was thin and lean now blossoms and, within a few months' time, develops physically into a fully matured woman. How this happens, how the fetus and the placenta are developed, and how various problems and complications should be treated are already described in a number of books. But so far no book has been published in which the mother-to-be can see and understand, week by week, the wonder which is taking place inside her.

After many years of work in cooperation with some of Sweden's gynecological clinics, Lennart Nilsson presents these astonishing photographs, which give an artistic as well as accurate and realistic picture of a human being's physical development from the moment of conception until birth. Here, step by step, parents can follow the different stages of fetal development. They learn when the different organs are formed, when the heart begins to beat, when the small arms and legs begin to move, etc. In this way the new life, which takes shape hidden from the world, becomes vivid and more easily perceived as a new and independent individual.

Lennart Nilsson's clear and revealing picture of human life in the womb is intended not only for the expectant mother—and father—but also for the general public, whose knowledge of this subject is often hazy. Many erroneous ideas are still common, for instance the notion that the fetus does not "come to life," as we often say, until about the middle of the pregnancy. Actually it is a living being from the very moment of conception.

Stockholm, September 1965   *Axel Ingelman-Sundberg*

Acknowledgments

Without the indulgent help and the great consideration I have had from many doctors, the pictures in the book could not have been taken. The positive attitude of these doctors toward the work, which has been going on for many years, has encouraged me to continue, and I am eternally grateful to them. Unfortunately it would take up too much space to mention them all. I want, however, to mention a few. First and foremost, Professor Axel Ingelman-Sundberg of the Women's Clinic at the Sabbatsberg Hospital. At the same hospital, Docents Mirjam Furuhjelm, Erik Odeblad, and Björn Westin as well as Doctors M. G. Gelli, Bertil Hagström, Carl Gustaf Lagergren, Rune Nyberg, and Gösta Åström have been of enormous help.

Other doctors, hospitals, and institutions that have been extremely important in the making of these pictures are Senior Physician Docent Harald Johansson and Doctors Björn Bjersner and Lars Hultgren at the Danderyd Hospital; Dr. Claes Wirsén at the Karolinska Institute; Professor Ulf Borell, Docent Jan Lindsten, and Doctors Maj Hultén and Birger Josephson at the Karolinska Hospital; Senior Physician Dr. Verner Westberg, Docent Jan Asplund, and Doctors Bertil Arpi and Arne Wikman at St. Erik's Hospital; Professor Herbert Swanberg and Dr. Sten Borgedahl at the Southern Hospital; as well as Researcher Tryggve Gustafson and laboratory assistant Ulla Hammar at the Wenner-Gren Institute.

Last but not least, I want to thank all the nurses who, with never-failing interest and patience, answered all my telephone calls and helped me in a variety of practical matters.

Lennart Nilsson

CONTENTS

A Child Is Born

The unborn child is a person no one knows. Is it a boy or a girl, is it blond or dark-haired? It has no name and no face. Even its mother knows very little: it is active and kicking or the calm and even-tempered type. People around her see only a pregnant woman.

The child just born is a son or daughter, an individual who will soon have a name and a place in the family. "It's a boy," announces the doctor (or midwife), lifting up a red, squalling little creature. "It's a boy," says the proud father to happy grandparents on the phone, while the newly delivered mother is busy counting fingers and toes and arms and legs over and over again. Her dream of a fair-haired daughter in a frilly party dress disappears at the sight of a wistful little old man crowned with a tuft of black hair. Or perhaps father's dream of a little boy for whom he would buy a toy train vanishes as he peers at a delicate young lady who already knows how to sneeze and yawn with decorum. Imagine, this particular child grew from one of the thousands of eggs in her and one of the millions of sperm in him. . . . And the father, cautiously letting the little fist grasp his own huge finger, wonders—as all fathers have wondered—how this well-shaped child could have come from almost nothing, how he himself, so detached from what has just happened, could have a part in every cell of this little human being.

How did it become a boy? Why is his hair black and not light? How could the fingers know that they were to be fingers, the hand that it was to be a hand?

How could one single cell, until then stored quietly in the body, suddenly give rise to a new human being with every feature that human beings have in common but still not exactly like any other living individual?

The child that became a boy doesn't wonder. It has no words for that yet. After all, it has been one and the same individual all this time, ever since the fertilized ovum began to divide into several cells. Everything has formed, grown, and developed in due time.

For several months this child has grasped, kicked, twitched at sudden sounds, sucked its thumb, slept, and waked again. Today it came out into the world. From now on it will have to breathe and eat by itself.

Having a baby is not something that happens in the course of one day at the hospital. The child has been around for many months, at first indicating its existence only by small external signs. Then the strange, small being grew and grew and changed the lives around it—not only that of the expectant mother, in whom all this happens, but also of the future father, who has to get used to being something entirely new, a father, even though nothing has changed within him.

This book is the story of their life during this time—theirs and that of their unborn child.

The Sea—Cradle of Life

When two people fall in love, marry, and have children, it is nothing new, however miraculous it may seem to them that they ever did meet in the turmoil of the world. Perhaps we had better not deprive the young couple of their illusions as they stand there making plans for the future. The main reason for the desire between man and woman has quite probably never occurred to them. It is simple and inescapable: in spite of civilization and millions of years on land, human life is still created and, in a sense, is spent in the waters of the sea.

All living organisms on earth consist of cells—some of only one cell, such as the amoeba. Most consist of millions of cells, each adapted to a special function and organized together with other cells to form various tissues and organs. When the first cells appeared on earth, the cooling primeval ocean provided the only habitable element. These one-celled organisms multiplied simply by dividing. Later on, when cells did not separate from each other after having divided, there arose multicellular organisms. While the water still covered our continents, all the biochemical processes

that we know as life were perfected. All the tissues in our body—
muscles, skeleton, nervous and circulatory systems, respiratory,
digestive, and reproductive organs and hormone glands—had in
principle attained their final form when the first species left the sea
waters to live on land.

But all individuals still began with a one-cell stage. To become
multicellular, organisms had to reserve certain cells that could
develop into new individuals. Even in very primitive species there

13

are two kinds of primordial, or germ, cells—the male and female—that must fuse to produce a new individual. Since this seems to be the most effective way of bringing variation into the genetic scheme of things, it has not altered much throughout the history of evolution. The difference between the sex cells of the sea urchin and those of man is astonishingly small.

All land animals still live in a kind of primeval ocean. They carry it inside themselves. Every cell inside the body floats in salt water, in which nourishment is dissolved and waste products are excreted. An outer covering, or integument, with hair, feathers, or scales has been given land creatures to protect them from drying out. But neither ova nor sperm have such a protective skin. Like other cells, they must float in salt water. Their joining together—the fertilization—and the early development of the new individual must still take place, as it were, in the primeval sea.

The most primitive animals need not fall in love. They just extrude their sex cells into the surrounding water without ceremony. This *external fertilization* is practiced by species living in colonies or shoals, such as corals or jellyfish. It is also seen in higher animals, up to fishes and amphibians, but among these it often becomes more complicated. In some species the ova are produced only on certain occasions, when the males might be far away. Therefore, many such creatures have developed elaborate courting performances to get together in pairs, and there may be violent fights between suitors about the honor of fertilizing the spawn. But for numerous other marine species intimate contact between male and female is an absolute prerequisite for making new individuals. This is true whenever the female of the species does not expel the eggs until after they have been fertilized.

In land animals such *internal fertilization* is necessary, for the primeval ocean exists only within them. The ova do not move, but lie within the female, waiting. The sperm, which find their way to the ova by swimming, must be delivered inside the female's body.

Reptiles and birds give their fertilized eggs a shell so that the small reservoir of salt water will not dry up while the young develop outside their mother's body. Mammals, however, stay and complete their development in the womb, in the fetal waters—the primeval sea.

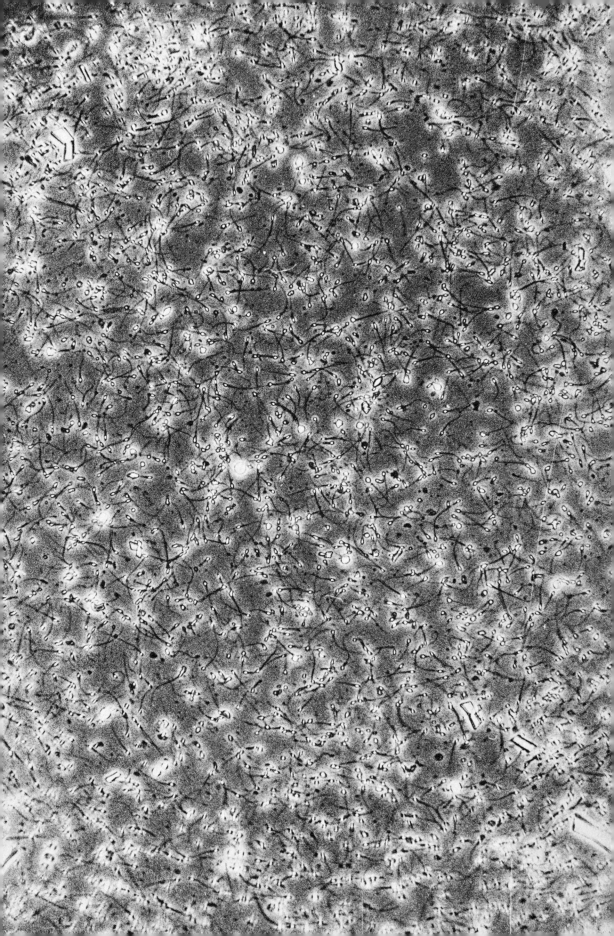

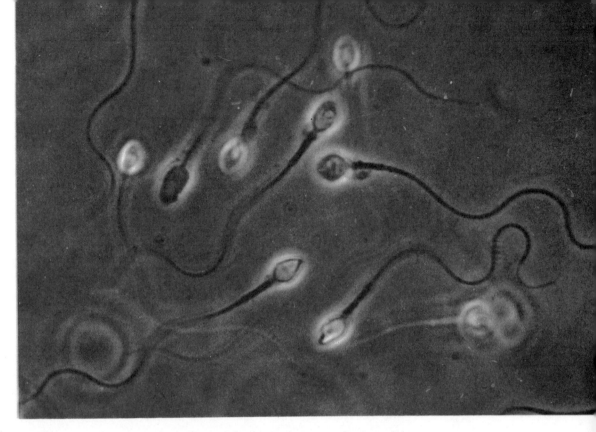

These are sperm seen in the microscope. The head, the midpiece or body, and the long tail, constantly whipping from side to side, can easily be distinguished. In view of the enormous numbers produced, it is no wonder that every one of them is not completely perfect. Even in the semen of healthy men, sperm retaining superfluous cytoplasm (lower left) or carrying two heads (lower right) may be present. However, with a sufficient number of normal sperm, the chances for conception are good.

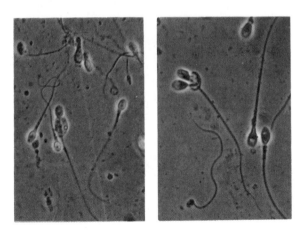

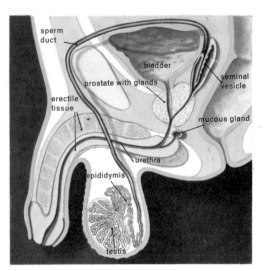

Millions of Sperm

Someone has calculated that enough ova to provide the present world population could be put in a top hat. The sperm to fertilize these three billion ova could be kept in a thimble! As much as a hundred million sperm per cubic centimeter of semen may be ejaculated by a healthy male at one time, the average volume of semen amounting to about 3 cubic centimeters. From puberty to old age, sperm are continuously developing in the tiny coiled tubules (known as seminiferous ducts) of the testes. Along the duct lining lie the sperm-producing cells. At short intervals they bud into new generations of cells. By two special forms of division the genetic material is blended and redistributed. Four "great-grand-children" thus appear in each litter produced by the millions of precursor cells. These will eventually develop into sperm, each containing its special mixture of the future father's characteristics. Since the cell generations lie piled up toward the center of the ducts, the fresh sperm need only loosen their attachment to be transported to the large coiled tube of the epididymis.

A sperm consists of a little package, as it were, of concentrated genetic material—the oval or round "head"—and a short body with cell organelles that can assimilate fuel to drive the long thin tail that the sperm uses for swimming. But it can't swim yet. First it will have to spend a week or two in the epididymis in order to mature.

When excited sexually, the male genital apparatus must produce, in only a few minutes, an ejaculation complete with lively sperm and nutritive fluid. The path the sperm will travel must be lubricated, and acid urine, if present, must be neutralized; the sperm are very sensitive to acid. The erectile tissue of the penis fills with blood and stiffens so that the penis can enter into the vagina. A few hundred million sperm, not yet moving under their own power, are rapidly mobilized from each epididymis and transported through the sperm ducts to the posterior part of the urethra. There the glands of the prostate have already deposited their secretions, containing substances to stimulate the sperm as well as others that are believed to influence the motility of the uterine musculature and thus help in the migration of the sperm. The last addition to the semen is the sugar-rich fluid from the seminal vesicles which provides fuel for the long swim. Along the whole urethra, small glands secrete a slightly alkaline lubricant. Then comes the orgasm: by means of vigorous, rhythmic muscular contractions the semen is ejected through the straight and stiff urethra, up into the vagina, toward the mouth of the uterus.

From then on the sperm have to move by themselves. They must still travel nearly eight inches to reach the place where the egg lies waiting. Even if they receive help—and quite a lot of help—to get there, eight inches is quite a distance for such a tiny thing, only about 60 microns long (one micron=.000039 of an inch). Many sperm succumb while still in the vagina, and not more than perhaps a hundred arrive in the neighborhood of the ovum. Of these, only one (out of the original few hundred million) reaches its destination. Only one penetrates the ovum's innermost envelope to fertilize it— if there is an ovum there. The woman who is to bear the child must first have provided a bed for it in her womb. If the ovum is not fertilized, this welcoming bed—the uterine lining—is shed and must be renewed. Only every four weeks is it ready.

One Ovum a Month

In view of the enormous number of sperm produced in the testes of the male, one ovum every four weeks may seem rather modest. Of course every ovum must have time to mature, to increase in volume, so that it will contain sufficient material for the first cells of the new individual. Each ovum matures within a small sac in the ovary known as a follicle. But there is much more than the ovum at stake. Every month the uterine lining must be rebuilt and ready to receive a new life. Each time this happens, a new hormone gland must be formed (the outer wall of the ovarian follicle) to stimulate the rebuilding of the uterine mucous membrane after each menstrual bleeding. The hormones, *estrogens*, from this follicle also make the

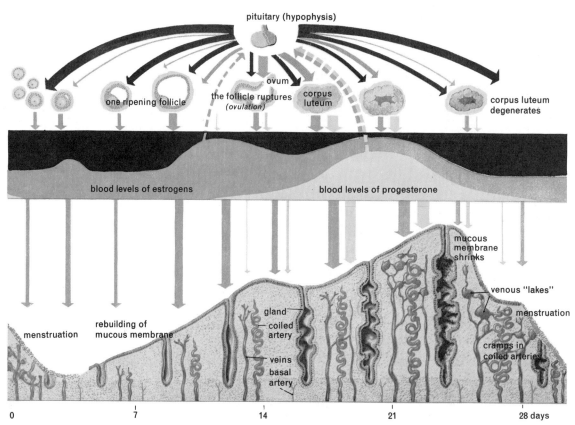

pituitary (hypophysis)

one ripening follicle

the follicle ruptures
(ovulation)

ovum

corpus
luteum

corpus luteum
degenerates

blood levels of estrogens   blood levels of progesterone

mucous
membrane
shrinks

venous "lakes"

menstruation

gland
coiled
artery

cramps in
coiled arteries

menstruation   rebuilding of
mucous membrane

veins
basal
artery

| 0 | 7 | 14 | 21 | 28 days |

Copyright Ciba. Ciba Collection of Medical Illustrations by Frank H. Netter, M.D.

→ follicle stimulating
   hormone (FSH)
⟹ corpus luteum stimulating
   (luteinizing) hormone
⟹ follicle hormone
   (estrogens)
⟹ corpus luteum hormone
   (progesterone)

Broken arrows signify hypothetic inhibitory action of ovarian hormones on the pituitary ("feedback" mechanism)

The menstrual cycle. The pituitary gland, a small organ the size of a bean and hanging down on a thin stalk at the base of the brain, secretes stimulating hormones into the blood. One of these hormones stimulates ripening follicles, and with the aid of a second hormone eventually causes one of the follicles—seldom two or more—to rupture and release the ovum. After that the collapsed follicle is transformed into the *corpus luteum*, producing estrogen (follicle hormones) and progesterone (the corpus luteum hormone). Blood levels of the ovarian hormones are shown in blue (estrogens) and yellow (progesterone). The estrogens promote the rebuilding of the uterine mucous membrane after each menstrual bleeding, and progesterone from the corpus luteum starts the secretion from the glands and prepares the superficial layers for the implantation of the fertilized ovum. If fertilization does not occur, the corpus luteum ceases to produce its hormones; that is, its action is triggered but not maintained by the pituitary. The coiled arteries are drawn into cramplike spasms and the mucous membrane begins to die. When after a day or two the cramps are relaxed, blood rushes through this tissue in decay, as it were, and the uterine lining is shed in the menstrual bleeding.

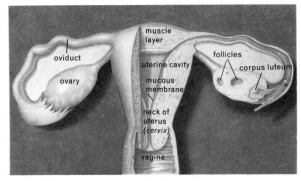

oviduct

muscle
layer

follicles

corpus luteum

ovary

uterine cavity

mucous
membrane

neck of
uterus
(*cervix*)

vagina

movement of the oviduct livelier, as it hovers over the surface of the ovary with its large, funnel-shaped opening to be sure to catch the ovum when it is released around the fourteenth day of the cycle. Small cilia (hairlike projections) in the oviduct keep a stream of fluid from the abdominal cavity moving down through the oviduct. There the ovum and the sperm will meet.

After fertilization, the new being floats in the oviduct on its way to the uterine cavity, where it will be implanted in the lining. This takes nearly a week, the last few days being spent in the uterine cavity. During this week the inner cell layer of the ruptured follicle forms the next part of the hormone gland, which is now called the *corpus luteum* (Latin for "yellow body"). The corpus luteum secretes a second type of ovarian hormone, progesterone, which, together with the estrogens, stimulates the uterine lining to provide nourishing fluid and prepare a welcoming bed for the fertilized ovum.

As a protective measure against the dangerous outer world, the glands of the cervix secrete a tough plug of mucus. But at the time the ovum is ready to be fertilized, estrogens from the follicle will, for about one day, change the plug into a smooth, half-fluid, glassy stream, in which the sperm can travel toward the waiting ovum.

Maturation into Man and Woman

The sex cells—eggs and sperm—are said to derive from some of the first cells of the body. When the new individual is still a seemingly shapeless cell mass of a few hundred cells, each of these may give rise to any part of the body, i.e., their exact fate is not yet determined. The same versatility is necessary for sperm and eggs if after their fusion they are to form all kinds of tissues and organs in the new individual.

At an early multicellular stage certain cells become separated from the rest and are stored near the place where, later on, the differentiation of the sex glands will occur. The "reserved" cells will then migrate into the future ovarian or testicular tissue, where they begin to multiply. Thus several generations of future sex cells are formed before birth.

In the male this multiplication continues after the beginning of

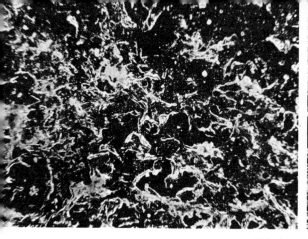

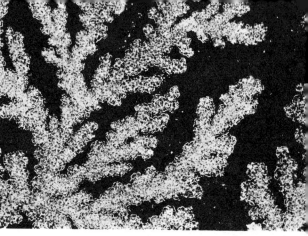

7th day

9th day

14th day

The Cervical Mucus

During the major part of the menstrual
cycle the cervical mucus is thick
and viscid. But in the middle of the
cycle, at ovulation time, it becomes
smooth and half fluid and may be
drawn out in long threads. The same
phenomenon occurs, remarkably enough,
at the beginning of the menstrual
bleeding. These changes are related to,
among other things, water content, which
is then at its highest in the smooth
mucus. If a drop of mucus is put on a
glass slide and cautiously heated, more
or less regular crystal patterns are seen
under the microscope as the mucus
dries. These patterns reach a maximum
at ovulation, when the mucus is thin,
watery, and easily penetrated by
the sperm. This simple test makes it
possible to follow the different phases
of a menstrual cycle.

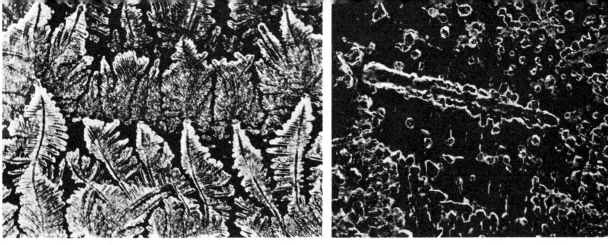

11th day

17th day

puberty, as the pituitary gland sends out stimulating hormones to the genital glands. These hormones "wake up" cells in the testes that are to produce the male sex hormone, testosterone. The boy grows into a young man with coarse body contours, a beard, and a deep voice. The sperm-producing ducts of the testes develop as well. For the rest of his life a large store of sperm-producing cells will distribute the genetic material present in the first cells of his body to millions and millions of sperm.

In the female the primordial sex cells will not multiply beyond the number present at birth, around 400,000. A number of these will probably succumb before puberty. At puberty the same pituitary hormones that stimulated the testicular tissue in the boy will promote estrogen secretion in the young girl from a large number of ripening follicles at one time. The girl is turning into a young woman. But, inhibited by ovarian hormones, the pituitary ceases stimulating the follicles. These shrink and degenerate. The pituitary then starts stimulating again; this "hormone pendulum" swings in a wider and wider arc, until one follicle, of the many stimulated, reaches full maturity at every period. The rest degenerate and are not used again. The luteinizing hormone from the pituitary causes the mature follicle to rupture, to release the ovum, and to be transformed into the corpus luteum, which secretes estrogens and progesterone. These hormones prepare the uterine lining to welcome the fertilized egg. But—presumably because of the rising levels of progesterone in the blood—the pituitary becomes silent again. The fate of the *corpus luteum*, and consequently that of the uterine lining, is at stake. Its doom is sealed on the twenty-eighth day. But even as the uterine lining is shed in the deluge of menstrual bleeding, the pituitary is already calling for new follicles to ripen.

In this way most of the primordial egg cells are discarded during the menstrual cycles, which proceed as long as there are any follicles left. The last egg cells in the last follicles ripening under stimulation from the pituitary will thus have been waiting for more than forty years.

The male: a level production of millions and millions of sperm, from puberty to old age, always ready to leave his body at short notice on the chance of fertilizing one single ovum.

The female: a four-week cycle, continuously repeated, of follicle maturation—rebuilding of the uterine lining—ovulation—preparations to receive the egg—degeneration of the corpus luteum—menstrual bleeding. This entire cycle takes place about 400 times during the fertile period, from early teens to middle life.

And yet in many ways the man and woman are not so different. Both have sex glands which fulfill the dual task of producing germ cells and of synthetizing male or female sex hormones to keep the delicately tuned mechanism going. The difference consists in their way of reacting as the pituitary sends out its stimulating hormones to the blood during early puberty. In him, balance and constant readiness; in her, a continuous swing between preparation and destruction.

The pituitary is situated very close to that part of the brain where the emotions are controlled and where the brain's own control centers are located. The swings of the "hormone pendulum" are probably regulated from these centers. No wonder, then, that moods also swing, and that the harmonious workings of this system are sensitive to anxiety or anticipation, grief or happiness.

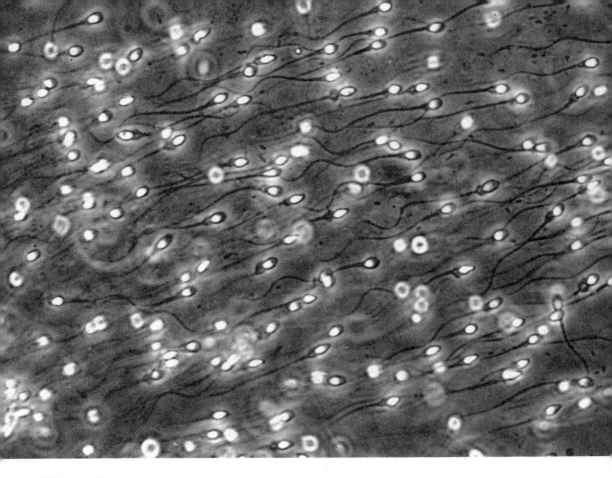

The Long Journey

Traveling over these two pages is an army of sperm, swimming eagerly in straight ranks. The tails stream behind and the heads show the direction of movement as they swim through the glassy, fluid cervical mucus on about the fourteenth day of the menstrual cycle—the day the ovum enters the oviduct.

Things do not go as well for sperm that appear at the wrong time. They have difficulty penetrating the viscid mass of mucous molecules, which constitutes an effective barrier during the greater part of the cycle (2 and 3). Even under ideal circumstances, the ranks of those able to proceed is constantly thinning out (4), and many die without having entered (5).

2

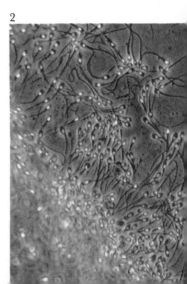

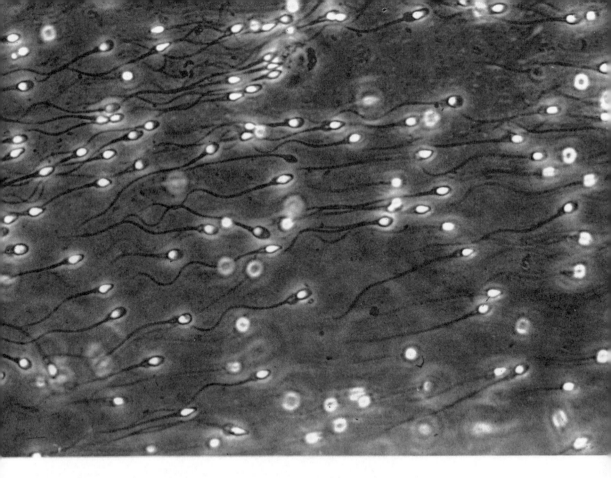

We cannot see the molecular coils characteristic of the mucus at ovulation, which give the large fernlike crystal patterns. But we know that they are present because of the regular arrangement of the penetrating sperm. The long molecules of the mucus are coupled together by transverse bindings; this explains why the

3   4   5

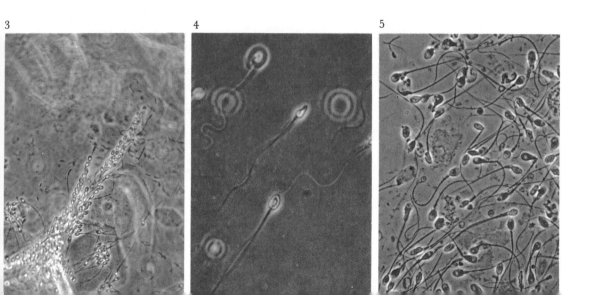

mucus can be drawn out in long threads as the molecules slide along each other. At 98.6°F. (normal body temperature) the molecules cannot lie still. They are constantly oscillating and the bindings sometimes become loosened for a moment. Then a sperm can take the opportunity to swim forward in free space as far as possible. It is rather like running the gantlet. When one is as small as a sperm, one has to pay attention to molecules and their position. The penetration of sperm in the cervical mucus is very much like the progress of a fleet of small boats up a river full of invisible logs.

According to present concepts, the sperm need not swim all the way, however. Some have been found in the outer part of the oviduct long before they could possibly have reached there by themselves. Some scientists contend that the sperm are in some way sucked into the uterus by movements in the uterine musculature. Their swimming power will be useful soon enough when they must search for the waiting ovum.

For the great majority of sperm the way up through the uterus and the oviduct is the road to destruction. Millions succumb in the acid secretions of the vagina. Presumably half of those which reach the uterine cavity enter the wrong oviduct. The rest run the risk of swimming astray in the labyrinth of folds and recesses in the widest part of the oviduct, where the ovum awaits their arrival.

There has been much speculation as to how the sperm find their way to the hiding place of the ovum. When observed in glass tubes, sperm have a tendency to swim upstream; they must swim against the stream of fluid which runs, due to the action of cilia, from the abdominal cavity toward the uterus. Apparently the ovum sends out some attracting substances as well, so that the sperm bear straight toward it. A few hours' sojourn in the oviducal secretion appears to be essential; if an unfertilized ovum is placed among sperm that have not been within the uterus or oviduct, the interest on the part of the sperm is not very impressive.

After ovulation the ovum is capable of being fertilized for only about twenty-four hours, perhaps even fewer. But sperm are patient suitors. They can endure for at least a couple of days. Meanwhile they find nourishment in the secretion that fills the oviduct.

The big cell that is extruded from the rupturing follicle on the day of ovulation is, strictly speaking, not really an ovum, but an egg-producing cell, corresponding to the sperm-producing cells in the male. Like these it passes through two special divisions to mix and redistribute the genetic setup from the future mother. Will this mean quadruplets?

No. In any case, quadruplets are not made that way. The enormous cell volume of the egg-producing cell, which makes it a giant among ordinary body cells, is needed to provide material for the first cells of the new individual. Therefore it is too precious to be divided among four equal parts. The first division, which occurs at the rupture of the follicle, does not go through the center but at the edge, and results in one big and one very small daughter cell. The latter is called the *polar body* and lies beside the big daughter cell inside the protective envelope. Polar bodies are sterile and cannot be fertilized. The next division, which gives rise to the ovum proper plus another polar body, starts immediately but is believed to be completed only if a sperm is present. In this way a fresh ovum is guaranteed.

Thus from each egg-producing cell in the female there develops only one sex cell, whereas the male makes four sperm in every set of divisions. Each release of sperm from the male offers a few hundred million variations from his bountiful genetic code, while the female provides, at most, only 400 during her whole fertile life.

This is still quite a lot. The children born to the average family are counted in one-figure numbers, as a rule. Even with millions of possible choices, the final selection must end up with one sperm for each ovum. However, the selection of ovum and sperm takes place at a different stage for each. In the ovary several follicles at a time compete for full maturation. Ordinarily only one releases an egg. The selection of the sperm takes place in the vagina, uterus, and oviduct as they race to fertilize the ovum. Considering all the obstacles along the way, we may well imagine that the best man wins.

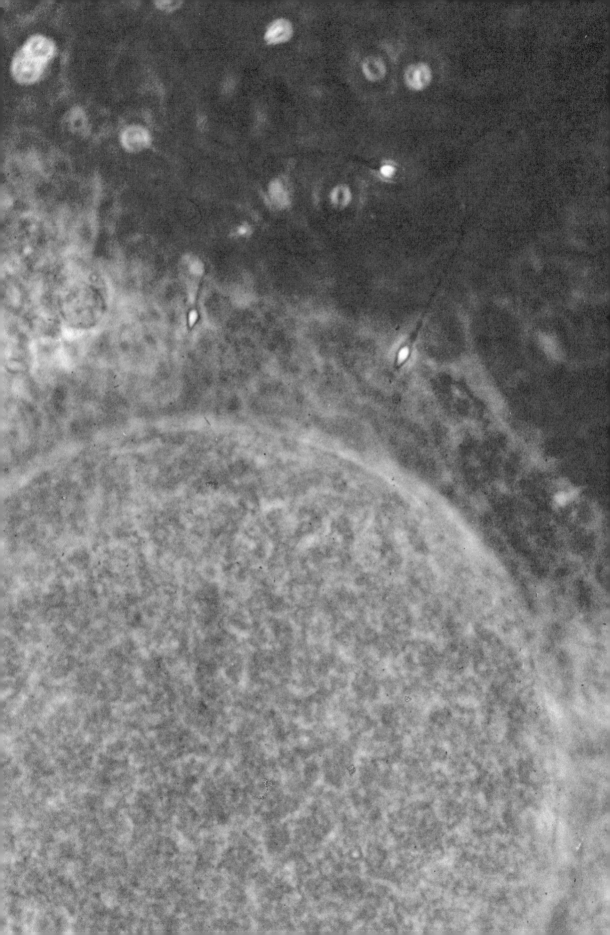

The First Encounter

The ovum is one of the largest cells in the body, its diameter measuring about .004 inch. It is thus just barely visible to the naked eye. It is surrounded by an envelope of follicle cells, a formation bearing the impressive Latin name *corona radiata,* the "radiate crown." The innermost cells of this formation have secreted a gelatinous coating during the maturation of the ovum, enveloping it within a kind of protective membrane.

As the ovum enters the oviduct the corona radiata cells soon become detached, permitting the sperm to come into closer contact. But the last obstacle—the gelatinous membrane—has yet to be overcome. This raises the crucial question: Which one of all the sperm is to fertilize the ovum?

One in a million finds the hiding place of the ovum—for this reason there has to be a sufficient number of sperm from the start. But still, the fusion of only one sperm and one ovum is needed for the creation of a new individual. When we look upon the relatively enormous ovum, surrounded by a number of small sperm eagerly exploring its surface, trying to penetrate its envelope from all directions, we begin to realize the importance of an efficient barrier. But this will suffice as an obstacle for only some of the sperm. When the strongest and liveliest sperm have bored their way through, the problem still remains: How will the ovum turn away all but one?

We do not yet know how this is accomplished in man and other higher animals, but there is always room for speculation. Boring through the gelatinous coat might be a relatively slow process. If so, one "nose length" could mean a start of a few minutes. The sperm that first comes into contact with the cell membrane of the ovum appears to be well received; we are told that in many species the membrane forms a cone that meets the sperm head and facilitates its passage into the ovum. Probably a simultaneous reaction takes place in the membrane which causes the sperm that follow to be turned away.

And so within the cytoplasm of the ovum the genes of the future parents prepare for their first encounter.

Chromosomes

These figures, which look like a swimming party in a prehistoric cave painting, are human chromosomes. Normally the chromosomes lie extended in the cell's nucleus as thin threads, but when the cell is going to divide, they contract into short rods, easily visible under a microscope.

Along the length of the chromosomes lie the hereditary units, or genes, arranged in a certain order. Each chromosome, during cell division, is split into two identical halves so that the genetic material can be equally distributed between daughter cells. Until division occurs the halves are held together at one single point. In the human being there are 46 chromosomes, or 23 pairs at the time the cell divides. As shown here, when each pair is lifted out of the large picture and arranged according to size, one of the 23 pairs doesn't match. This odd pair is the sex chromosomes, which in this individual consist of one big X chromosome and one small Y chromosome, that is, the chromosomes belonging to a male individual. The female has two X chromosomes in the 23rd pair.

It is natural, and correct, to conclude that one chromosome in each of the pairs comes from the mother and the other one from the father.

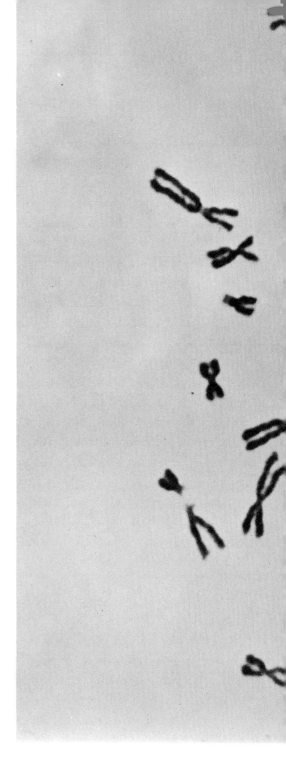

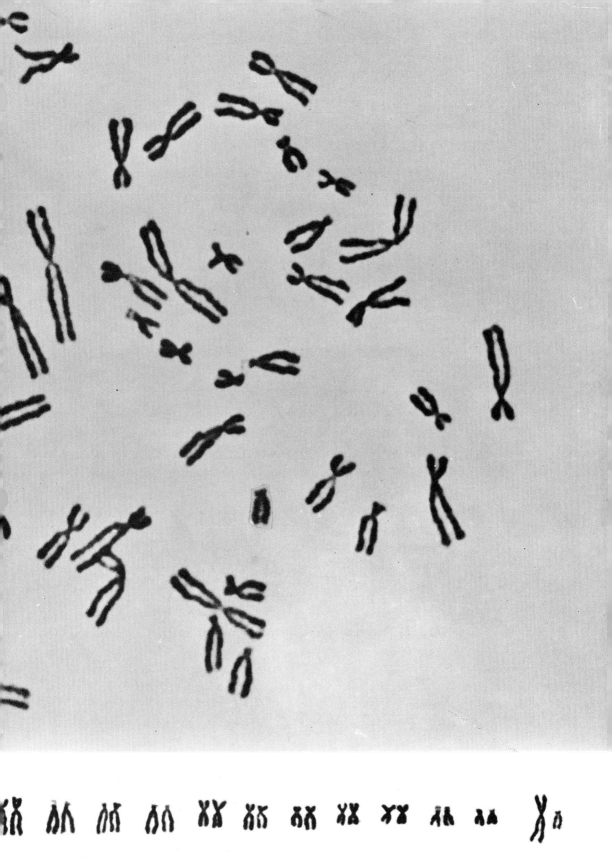

An ordinary cell division as seen in one of the chromosome pairs could be pictured as follows:

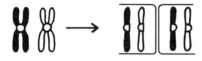

Each daughter cell gets a set of "half" chromosomes. Before the next cell division can take place, new halves must be made so that the chromosomes may split again. This is accomplished by duplicating the genetic material:

In this way the same genetic setup will prevail from one generation to another of new cells. We remain the same individuals throughout our lives, although a great many of our body cells wear out and are replaced by new ones.

But to our children we give only one of the chromosomes in each pair—they are to have one of each pair from their mother and one from their father. This is why the cells which are to give rise to sperm or ova must pass through their two special divisions.

The whole thing could be extremely simple. Instead of each dividing in half, the chromosomes in each pair could be separated in the first division:

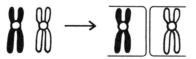

In the second division, the postponed splitting of the chromosomes could take place:

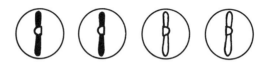

If we had only this pair of chromosomes, we could give birth to only two sorts of children—there wouldn't be much variety.

And even if we assumed that the pairs separate randomly, so that not all the chromosomes from the mother go to one daughter cell or all those from the father to the other daughter cell, all the millions of sperm and thousands of ova would still contain only different combinations of 46 chromosomes. It is theoretically possible that some couple might be able to announce the birth of "a copy of the first-born."

As matters stand, the likelihood is practically nil. Before the first division the chromosome pairs celebrate a kind of delayed wedding. Since each chromosome—except in the XY pair of a male individual—has a mate of the same size and with a similar arrangement of genes, a pairing may occur. During this pairing, whole sequences of genes may be exchanged before the chromosomes separate again at the first division. At the next division four different combinations may result from one pair:

As there are thousands of genes in each chromosome and thus thousands of exchange possibilities, and as chance seems to determine the results of this exchange in all pairs, an almost endless number of combinations is possible in the production of sperm and ova. Every individual (except monovular twins, triplets, etc.) is unique. At the same time, of course, this individual resembles his or her parents, for it is their genes that have been mixed. Also the children are born to be human beings, that is, their genes are arranged within 46 human chromosomes.

Now what about the sex chromosomes? Why is the child a boy? Or a girl?

That depends on the sperm. Since there are two X chromosomes in female cells, all ova contain one X chromosome. But male cells have a Y chromosome instead of one X, and so the maturing sperm will be of two kinds: some containing a Y chromosome, some not. There has been much discussion as to whether this is reflected in the form and function of the individual sperm, but no definite conclusions have yet been reached. As it happens, more male babies are born than female, and, judging from miscarriage and abortion statistics, still more appear to be conceived. It may well be that the proportion of X and Y sperm is not always 50-50. Some scientists maintain that the relationship in time between coitus and ovulation may be an important factor in determining the sex of the child. Whatever remains to be learned about the composition of human families, we may safely assume that sex is not determined at random.

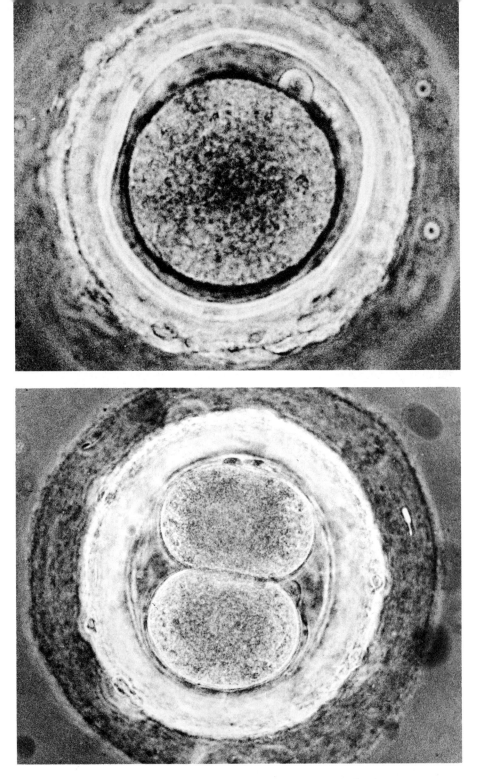

The first divisions after conception are noteworthy in two respects:
the length of the intervals between them—up to twelve hours—
and the practically constant volume in spite of the multiplication
of cells.

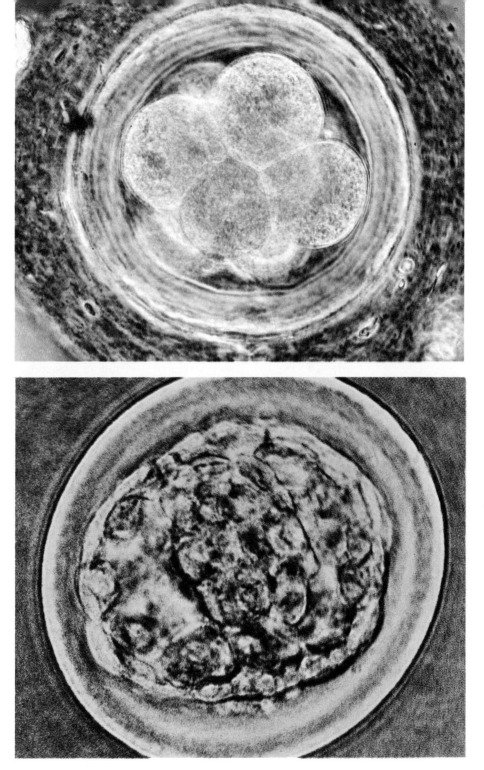

The cells get smaller and smaller, but the whole mass still has plenty of room inside the original envelope. It seems as though the first divisions only serve to make several small compartments out of the cytoplasm of the ovum.

During the first week of its existence the new being floats freely in the secretions from the oviduct and uterus on its way down into the uterine cavity. The passage from the oviduct is believed to be closed for a few days as the fertilized ovum divides and prepares to enter the uterus and be submerged in the uterine lining. The new creature drifting down toward the uterus is no shapeless mass, but an organized cluster of cells that have already begun to apportion different tasks among themselves.

This differentiation appears rather early. If all the cells were alike, they would probably divide simultaneously; there would be a 4-cell stage, an 8-cell, a 16-cell, etc. But stages with an odd number of cells have been observed. This implies that some cells divide faster than others. From a single cell, the fertilized ovum, there have emerged several kinds of cells. How does this agree with the fact that all cells—except sex cells—in the same individual have the same genetic setup?

The explanation is that each type of cell uses only its special part of the genetic code. Brown eyes and dark hair, for instance, are hereditary features. But this surely does not mean that all cells in the developing child get brown eyes and dark hair. These features are a matter of concern only for the pigment cells of the iris and the hair follicles. All other cells in that individual also carry these particular genes but pay no attention to them. Throughout the development of every living thing this selection prevails, resulting not in millions of copies of the ovum, but in a highly organized cell community in which every part has been given its special task.

For the moment, the most important job is not the making of the child; for some time the human embryo will remain a small cluster of cells inside a vesicle formed by those cells from the ovum that divide faster. These rapidly dividing cells will eventually attach the vesicle to the uterine lining, and then penetrate this lining to implant the developing embryo under its surface.

Pregnancy is counted from the first day of the last menstrual bleeding. The ovum is normally fertilized within a day of ovulation, around the fourteenth day of the cycle. During the first two weeks, then, the woman is actually not pregnant at all. Implantation generally occurs about seven days after fertilization, i.e., near the twenty-first day of the cycle. A week remains before the next menstrual bleeding is due. But the expectant mother suspects nothing.

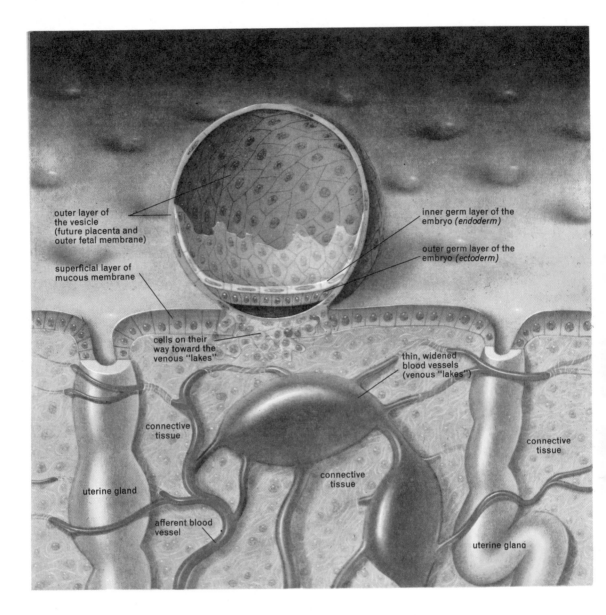

outer layer of
the vesicle
(future placenta and
outer fetal membrane)

inner germ layer of the
embryo (endoderm)

outer germ layer of the
embryo (ectoderm)

superficial layer of
mucous membrane

cells on their
way toward the
venous "lakes"

thin, widened
blood vessels
(venous "lakes")

connective
tissue

connective
tissue

connective
tissue

uterine gland

afferent blood
vessel

uterine gland

The embryonic vesicle lands with its precious load. The shapeless cell cluster, destined from the very beginning to form the origin of a new individual, has now developed into a round disk with two layers, the ectoderm and the endoderm. The embryo lands on its back, so to speak; thus the ectoderm becomes the lower layer. The endoderm is now spreading out against the vesicle wall, like a kind of wallpaper. Eventually there will be two vesicles, the new endodermic one inside the original vesicle. A hollow space is also forming below the embryonic disk. It may be hard to believe at this stage, but this small cavity will later on enclose the developing fetus in a kind of intrauterine swimming pool. Soon the whole vesicle will be submerged in the uterine lining—the cells of its outer layer are rapidly multiplying and penetrating downward to prepare the way.

41

The Second Week

The situation for the tiny new being is most precarious. For the mother it constitutes a foreign body which under other circumstances would be rejected immediately. The modest amounts of oxygen and nourishment provided by the uterine secretions will not suffice in the long run. In the usual course of events the corpus luteum would begin to degenerate. Within a week the whole uterine lining would be shed in menstrual bleeding.

But these impending dangers are averted by a combination of force and cunning, as it were. The cells on the outer layer of the vesicle are aggressive—the figure shows how they eat their way into the mucous membrane to penetrate the blood vessels full of oxygen and nourishment. The vesicle collapses and can be easily drawn down through the narrow hole excavated by the aggressive cells. When the surface closes over again, the vesicle expands under it and the outer cells continue to multiply and erode more and more blood vessels. The maternal blood will now stream freely through a thick, spongy layer which gathers up nourishment for the embryo: the developing placenta.

But force is no longer essential for these outer cells, which have come into contact with the maternal blood. They form instead a multi-nucleated coating that takes in oxygen and nourishment and carries away carbon dioxide and waste products. Peace will also be made with the surrounding maternal tissue. The blood-filled spaces will gradually expand, and within them the placental tissue will grow out in a network of little roots, known as the placental villi. This expansion will be greatest on that side of the vesicle which faces downward, toward the bottom of the mucous membrane. Toward the surface, the tissue will be extended as the vesicle grows; thus the villi will gradually be smoothed out. In this part, the smooth-surfaced outer fetal membrane, the *chorion,* will be formed.

Once the invasion has progressed this far, the uterus seems to accept the parasite that is sucking nourishment in its wall. But now some cunning will be required to coax the lining into staying there until the delivery, which is still thirty-seven weeks ahead. This coaxing is the job of the *corpus luteum*. This hormone gland must be stimulated from the pituitary to be able to furnish its estrogens and progesterone and thus maintain the uterine lining. But on account of the "feedback" mechanism previously mentioned, the stimulus from the pituitary is now withdrawn. This time the cells within the placental villi intervene. They secrete a hormone similar to that furnished by the pituitary and send it via the maternal blood to the *corpus luteum*. The latter, making no distinction as to the source, uses the hormone to maintain the uterine lining and the situation is saved, at least for a while. There will be no menstrual bleeding on the twenty-eighth day.

This hormone, named *chorionic gonadotropin* (abbreviated HCG— H for human), like many other hormones, is excreted in the urine. By the time the next menstruation fails to come, the urine begins to contain considerable amounts. Recently, technically simple methods to test the urine have been developed and the answer can be had within an hour. The urine sample is mixed with a solution of antibodies against HCG, to which is added a suspension of HCG-coated red blood corpuscles or latex particles. Normally the antibodies will react with the HCG coating, causing the corpuscles or latex particles to clump together. In the case of pregnancy, however, the antibodies will react to the HCG present in the urine instead, and the suspended particles float freely.

Long before there are any visible signs of pregnancy and before the diagnosis can be made by ordinary gynecologic examination, the new individual has made its presence known in the body. In spite of the fact that the little vesicle with its embryo and microscopic placenta is the size of the head of a pin, it has managed, hidden away beneath the surface of the uterine lining, to alter the hormonal pattern of the expectant mother. By the time the next menstruation should have come, the new individual is well established. The "child" itself is only a small round disk one-hundredth of an inch wide with one little vesicle on its back and one underneath. It does not look like very much, but during its third week the embryo will, thanks to its firm anchoring and efficient supply of nourishment, rapidly proceed in its development from a thin, two-layered disk to a rounded little body with head, trunk and umbilical cord.

The Third Week

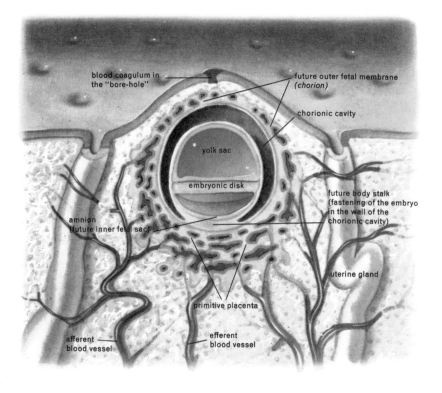

blood coagulum in the "bore-hole"

future outer fetal membrane (chorion)

chorionic cavity

yolk sac

embryonic disk

future body stalk (fastening of the embryo in the wall of the chorionic cavity)

amnion (future inner fetal sac)

uterine gland

primitive placenta

afferent blood vessel

efferent blood vessel

The embryo is now well established under the surface. The outer layer of the vesicle continues to grow and erode more blood vessels as well as uterine glands to get nourishment. In the lower figure, the chorionic cavity can be seen expanding in advance so that the embryo will have plenty of room to develop. Toward the bottom of the mucous membrane the placenta begins to form.

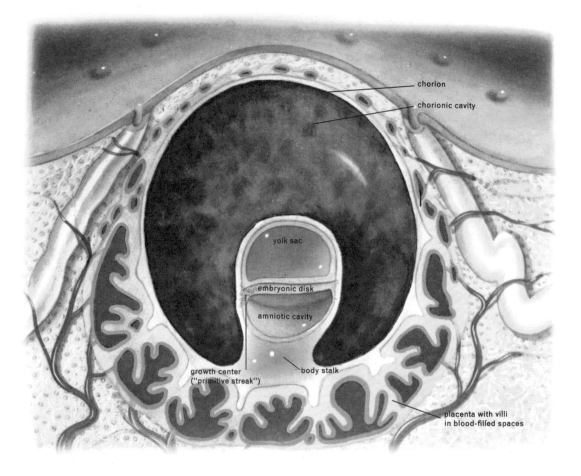

chorion

chorionic cavity

yolk sac

embryonic disk

amniotic cavity

growth center ("primitive streak")

body stalk

placenta with villi in blood-filled spaces

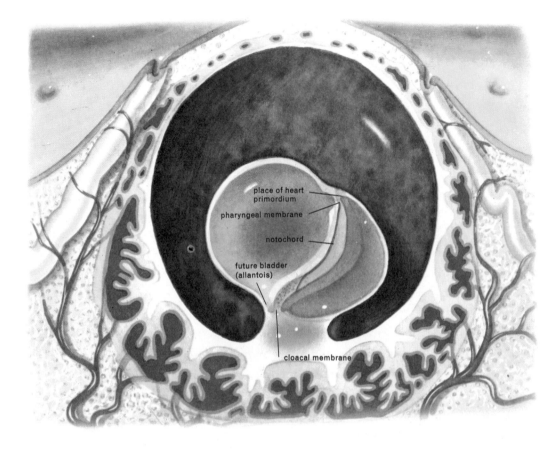

place of heart
primordium
pharyngeal membrane
notochord
future bladder
(allantois)
cloacal membrane

At first the embryo is but a two-layered disk. But toward the beginning of the third week a kind of growth center appears at one edge. The disk therefore continues to grow mainly longitudinally, and an axis appears between the germinal layers: the notochord. But the straight edge does not keep pace with the expansion of the disk. The embryo will soon bend over it in all directions; it spreads forward in a big rounded head end, and then it "sits down" over the hind border and grows a tail.

head bend
mouth (pharyngeal) membrane
pharynx (foregut)
mouth
heart
future rectum
(hindgut)
yolk sac stalk
allantois
cloacal membrane
tail bend

The Fourth Week

Not a very cute baby, this little embryo in its amniotic sac. Menstruation is now one week overdue. A blunt head end projects forward with a large, primitive mouth cavity just above the bulging heart—one could say that the embryo literally has its heart in its mouth. The other end of the body tapers off in a somewhat smaller and pointed tail.

At the bottom of the abdomen is the body stalk, now joining the yolk sac stalk to form an umbilical cord. This latter will eventually be enveloped in the amniotic sac (the inner fetal membrane). This sac will be expanded more and more by the fetal fluid until it covers the inner side of the chorion as if it had been glued to it.

In the beginning the umbilicus occupies the entire edge of the embryonic disk and keeps pace with its expansion. But soon the disk begins to grow faster, bending upward; it "arches its back." Growth is faster in the fore end, slower in the back end, and slowest on either side. The disk is thus transformed into an oval body with a large head, a short, slim tail, and not very broad sides. But the body continues to grow. It is as though a balloon were being inflated through the neck of the umbilical cord. Eventually there appears the rounded body of a baby with a cord attached to the middle of its belly (just as it should be).

The body wall now consists of three layers. The outer layer will form the epidermis, with hair, sebaceous and sweat glands, and the nervous system. The middle layer, in the axial part of which the notochord, predecessor of the spine, extends from the roof of the mouth to the root of the tail, will turn into the primordia of the corium and subcutaneous tissue, of muscles, skeletal bones, blood and lymph vessels, kidneys, and genital glands; and into connective tissue and various cell elements of the blood. Finally, there is an inner layer, the roof of the yolk sac. From this layer will develop the digestive tract with lining and glands, the urinary system, and the lungs. This specialization takes place remarkably fast.

The nervous system begins to form toward the beginning of the fourth week—the sixth week of pregnancy. The outer layer of the body wall thickens at the midline. Simultaneously two longitudinal folds appear on either side of the thickening. This creates a groove running between the two ends of the embryo. At its "waist" the edges of this groove curl and begin to fuse, making the groove into a tunnel. The fusion proceeds rapidly in both directions, and within a couple of days the groove is transformed into a long tube with only two narrow openings, or pores, one at either end. These pores soon close, the fore end swells to form the brain, and nerves begin to grow out from the brain stem and the primitive spinal cord.

Now a spine with vertebrae must begin to form. On either side of the tube, where fusion first began, the adjacent tissue begins to divide into a row of quadrangular segments. There will be more than 40 pairs in all. We develop from the head end downward. The trunk is not completely formed until the last pair of segments appears in the very tip of the tail. In a newborn, the head still comprises one quarter of the body length. But during growth this proportion changes until in the adult the head is only an eighth of the body length, the waist is placed just above the middle, and the legs are the longest part.

Out of more than 40 pairs of segments will be formed 32 to 33 vertebrae; not all the segments develop beyond the rudimentary stage. Muscle primordia form between the bodies of the vertebrae and between the ribs that are now protruding from the twelve thoracic vertebral primordia. Also in the spaces between the bodies of the vertebrae are nerve stems, working their way out from the developing spinal cord.

Between the primitive mouth opening and the heart, a face and a throat are beginning to form. Six projections grow out from each side, bending toward the midline where they join into arches, the uppermost pair first. It looks almost as if the baby were going to have gills. From the first arch the mandible, or lower jaw, is formed. A cleft in the middle of the chin is considered a sign of strength and energy. Actually it should be regarded as a mark of underdevelopment—the joint is showing.

By the fourth week of its existence the baby has the beginnings of a circulatory system. And one day in the beginning of that week a rudimentary heart starts beating.

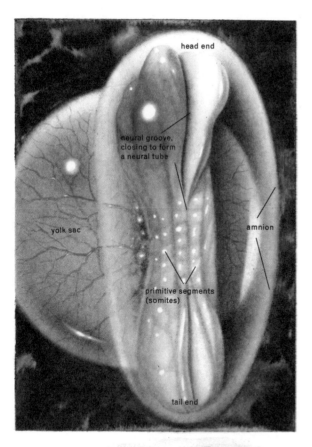

head end

neural groove, closing to form a neural tube

yolk sac

amnion

primitive segments (somites)

tail end

Viewed from the back, the bending of the embryo at both ends is shown. The primitive segments mark the appearance of a third germinal layer—the mesoderm—between the two original ones (endoderm and ectoderm).

26 days
total length ⅛ inch

Lower figure: 1. forehead; 2. eye; 3. mandible; 4. mouth and pharynx; 5. the three upper visceral, or neck, arches; 6. aorta; 7. heart; 8. future trachea; 9. esophagus; 10. future spine; 11. liver primordium; 12. veins; 13. umbilical cord; 14. future bladder; 15. rectum; 16. cloaca; 17. body stalk.

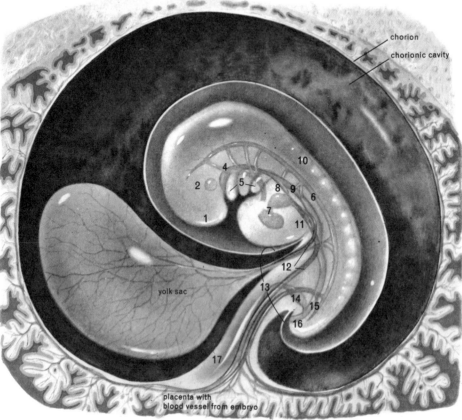

chorion

chorionic cavity

yolk sac

placenta with blood vessel from embryo

The Embryo—Fish or Fowl?

Around the thirtieth day of its existence, when the mother is in the middle of the second month of her pregnancy, the embryo has grown to about 1/5 of an inch, and is beginning to resemble a vertebrate. Even its loving mother, however, would not find it very like its parents.

But now the development accelerates. The baby grows about a quarter of an inch a week and looks more and more human. The heart pumps more and more blood through an expanding circulatory system that reaches into all parts of the placenta in an elaborate network like the tree of life. The chorionic cavity grows and causes the uterine lining to bulge into the uterine cavity, and the placenta spreads into new territories, where oxygen and nourishment stream in yet uneroded blood vessels.

It is often said that the development of the individual recapitulates the evolution of the species. We all start as one-celled beings. The sperm and ova of sea urchins and man are, at a hasty glance, strikingly alike. A fish embryo swims around with a yolk sac hanging down from its belly and also has six arches—gill arches—between the mouth and the heart. There is not even very much difference between the chick embryo in the egg and the human embryo in the chorionic cavity on the day when their hearts start beating, though it takes the chicken only two days to get to that point. Could it be that at an early stage the child is a fish or a frog or a young bird? When does the embryo in a human mother become a human being?

It has been one all the time, since the moment of conception. Of course it has several features in common with most living organisms, for all creatures have the same origin. During the first day of the human embryo's existence it was already determined that it was to be a multicellular organism; the ovum divided. During the fourth week vertebrate characteristics appeared. After about the seventh week, its appearance left no doubt that it was meant to develop into a human being. Although the earliest stages had much in common with those of other species, the future development was determined from the very beginning.

Now, what about the yolk sac? And the gill arches?

The similarity between the human embryo and the fish embryo consists in the fact that they both, being vertebrates, have the same early, primitive features. But they make different uses of them. The fish embryo, developing freely outside its mother, obtains its food supply from the yolk sac. The human embryo uses the yolk for making blood corpuscles. The fact that fish make gills out of their four inferior arches should not be taken as proof that we human beings pass through some kind of "fish stage" during our stay in the womb. We will breathe with lungs, and in addition to the mandible and hyoid bone a larynx will be formed from one of our six neck arches. As to how we and other higher vertebrates once developed from amoebas, fishes, and reptiles—that is a different story.

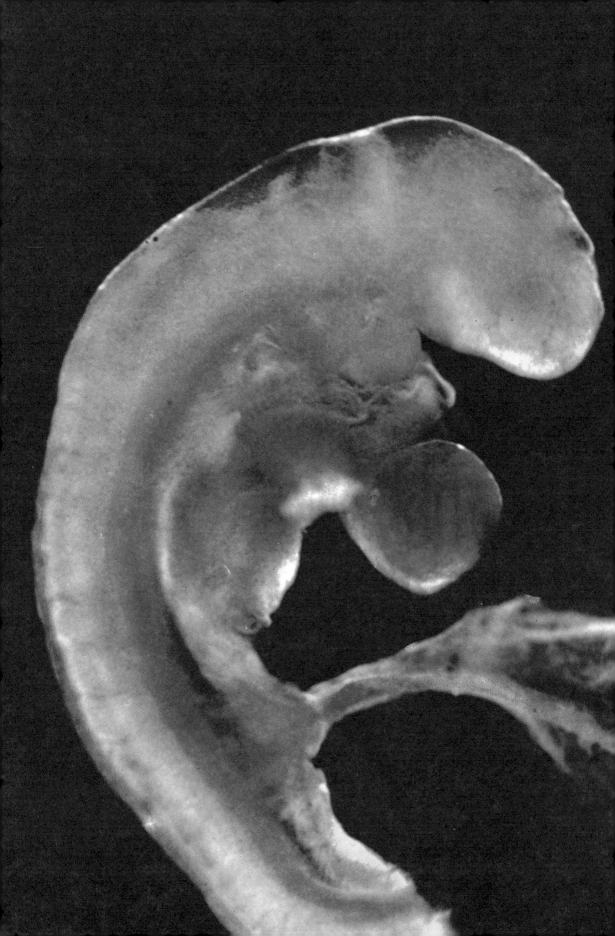

From Embryo to Fetus

1/6 of an inch, 28 days old. Six weeks of pregnancy have passed. The body is bent forward because the back grows faster. It is not yet easy to tell where the trunk ends and the head begins. There are no clearly marked extremities.

The blunt head end consists of the forehead with the foremost part of the brain. A faint oval is just visible on the surface: the developing eye. Below the forehead lies the primitive mouth cavity. Three red, shimmering protuberances are seen to the left of the mouth: these are the three upper "neck" arches, each with its blood-filled artery.

The heart is still a curved tube. The part which will develop into the ventricles is seen bulging far outside the body. It seems rather large for such a small embryo. But the blood vessels in the embryo are only a small part of the network through which the heart must pump the blood. Most of this network lies within the placenta.

The circulatory system inside the body is still very simple: one large aorta on either side with a branch through each of the "neck" arches, a couple of branches leading to the yolk-sac stalk and two through the umbilical cord for the placenta. The veins run back again the same way. For some reason the right aorta eventually shrinks and disappears, while the fourth arch on the left side continues to grow and forms the aortic arch from the heart to the straight portion of the aorta, the upper part of which is thus actually the original left main stem.

In the picture a large vessel is seen leading from the trunk to the yolk sac. On closer examination, horizontal segments along the back may be seen, gradually decreasing in size toward the tail. The fourth segment from the top lies at the same level as the heart. This is where the neck begins.

Next page:
30 days, 1/5 inch

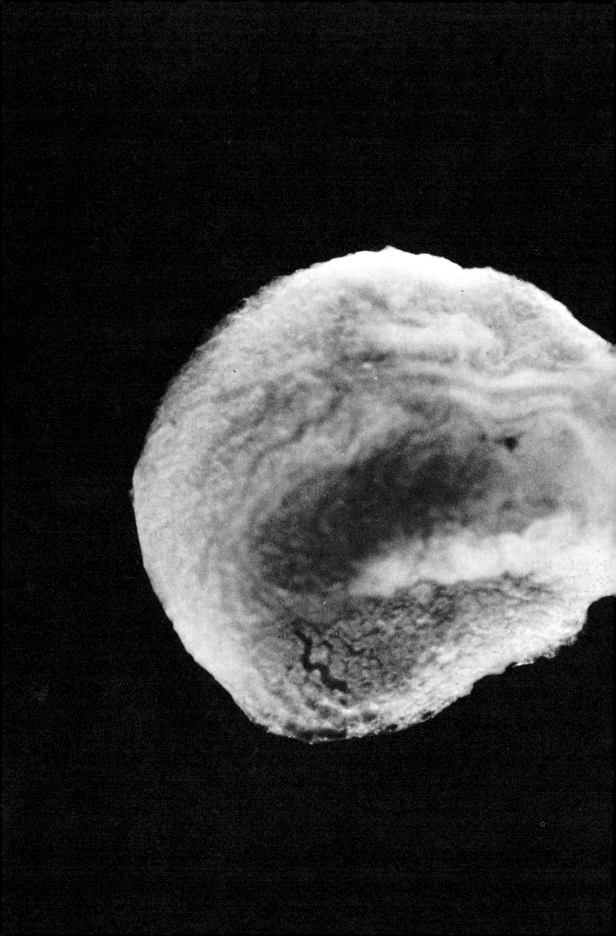

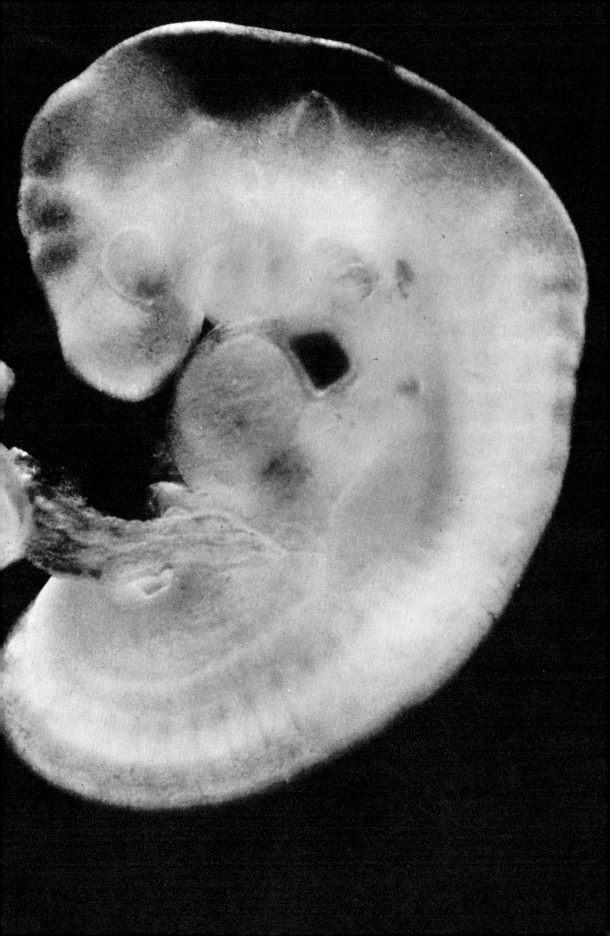

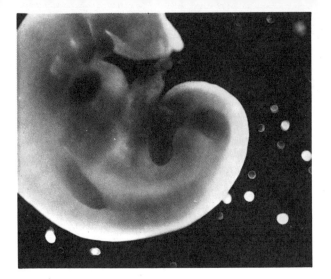

Fifth week after fertilization: A long dark crest has developed along the side of the trunk. At either end of this crest two oval patches are seen, one between the dark heart and the contour of the back, and the other close to the root of the dark, bent tail; these are the arm and leg buds.

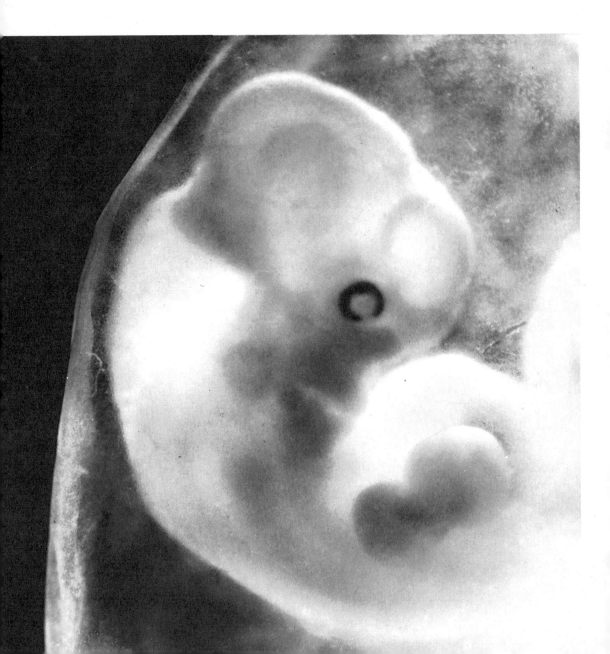

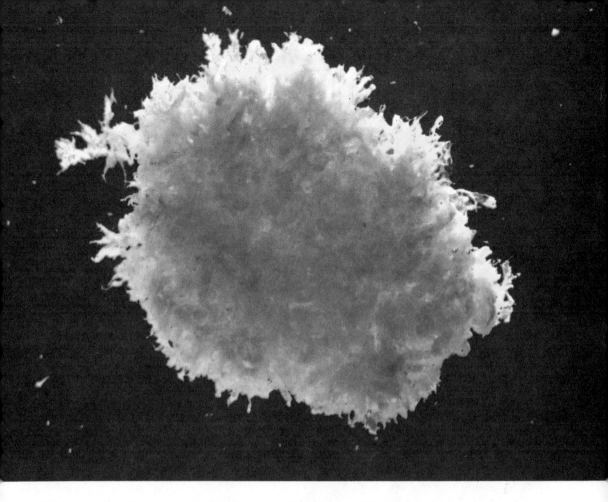

This is the exterior of the chorionic sac of the 28-day-old human being shown in the color picture facing page 53. The sac is not very large, only a little over an inch across. But with its thousands of thin radicles it has a considerable area for absorbing nourishment from the maternal blood streaming around it in the uterine lining.

The embryo to the left is just about to begin its sixth week and is consequently 35 days old. The eye is clearly seen as a black circle, incompletely closed; what appears is actually the edge of the fundus of the eye, which contains a black pigment. It looks as though the baby had a large mouth with thick lips beneath the eye. This is the outer ear, still placed quite low. The upper extremity bud has developed into a plump little paw. The upper arm and forearm are very short. What looks like the wrist is in fact the elbow.

57

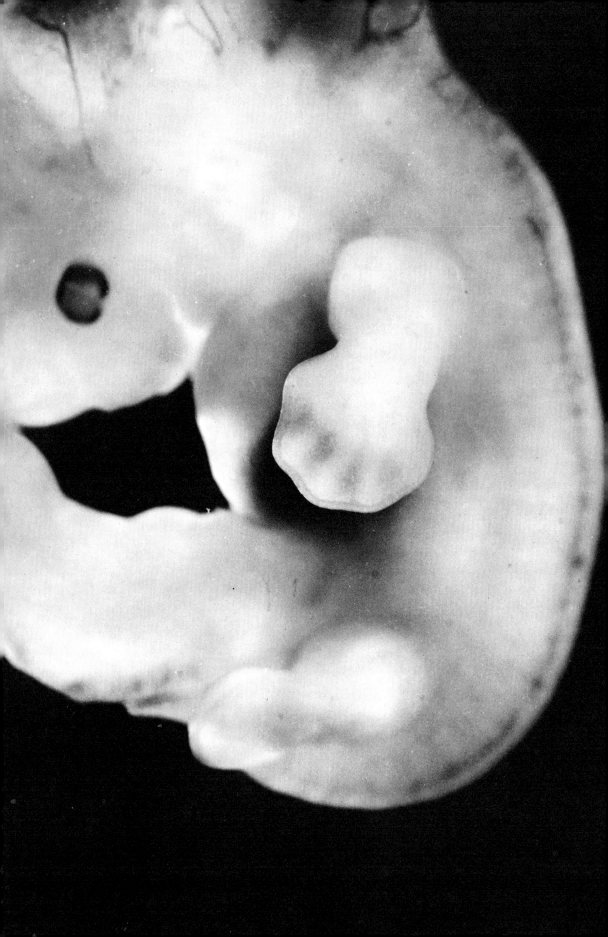

37 days old, ½ inch from crown to rump. There is not much body yet beneath the thick umbilical cord. The arm is far ahead of the leg in development, the head far in advance of the trunk.

This week, the sixth in the life of the baby and the eighth of pregnancy, is the period of design. Arms and legs, body and face, take shape as though sculptured from inside.

We do not know very much about the factors and forces that govern this process, that make the cells move into their right place without hesitation and start building up part of an arm or a leg without ever having done so before. There must, of course, be a certain organization within cell areas that determines the action of surrounding cells; it is known that orders are emitted from more developed centers to still shapeless clusters of cells. It is also believed that certain defined paths are staked out, that a kind of invisible pattern is present in the gelatinous mass, the *ground substance*, which fills out all the interstices of the primitive connective tissue in the middle layer of the embryonic body.

In the hand, five separate condensations have appeared, out of which the bones of the palm and the fingers will soon grow. A little later the same thing will happen in the foot, forming the metatarsal bones and the toes. As the arms and legs grow longer the hands and feet get farther away from the body.

In the middle of the face the frontal outgrowth, known as a "process"—which later on will become the nose and the middle part of the maxilla and upper lip—and the two cheek processes meet. During the following weeks the nasal septum will sink down and join the two palatal processes which are drawn up like gates from the side walls of the primitive mouth cavity and fuse in the midline. There will thus be a ground floor—the mouth cavity proper—with the palate as a roof, and a second floor—left and right nostril—with a longitudinal nasal septum in the middle. The molecules of the ground substance direct all the growing processes so that the fusion will occur in exactly the right place.

Along the sides of the trunk, cells are moving in twelve horizontal currents which will give rise to the ribs. They meet in the midline on the breast where they help form the sternum. Between the ribs, and in the trunk wall beneath the chest, future muscle cells are migrating. And just beneath the surface the skin is taking shape. The connective tissue of the subcutis and corium spreads from the back toward the front. The cells of the delicate outer layer start making the final epidermis with hair follicles and the sweat and sebaceous glands.

It is as though a single-breasted jacket were being slipped on under the thin surface—with a hole left for the umbilical cord.

Just over 5½ weeks, ½ inch

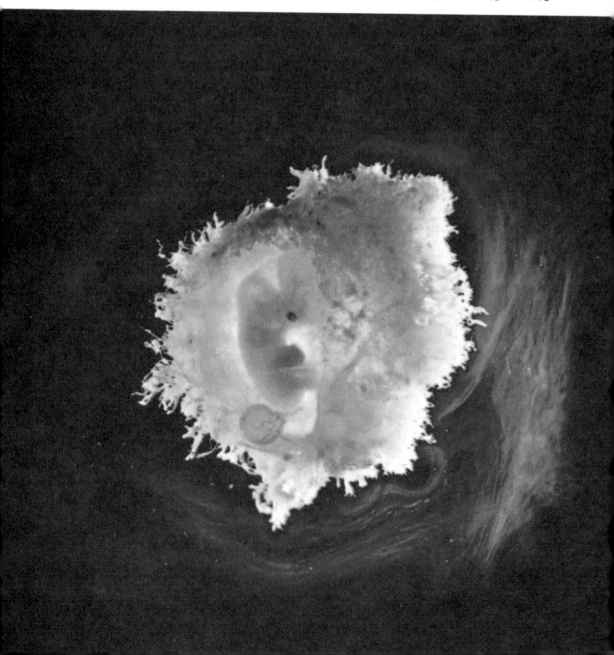

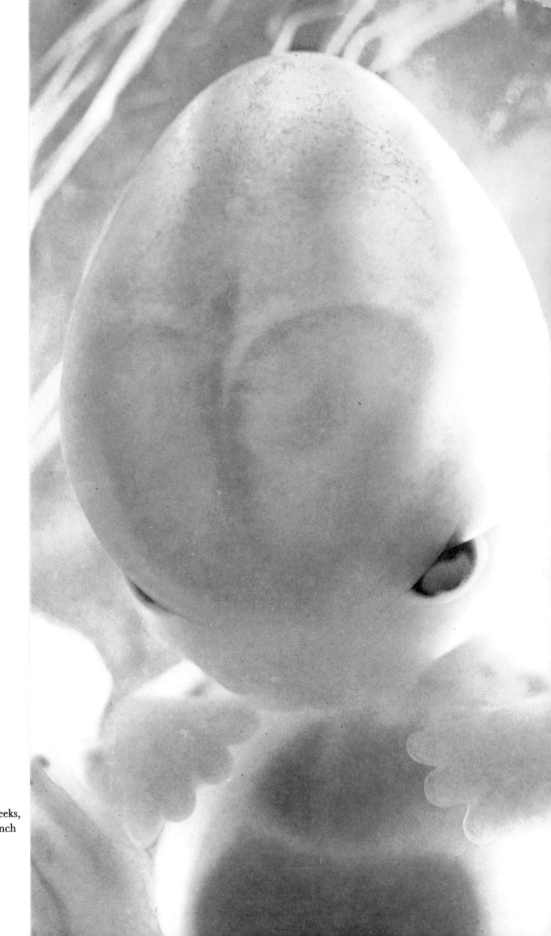

6 weeks,
½ inch

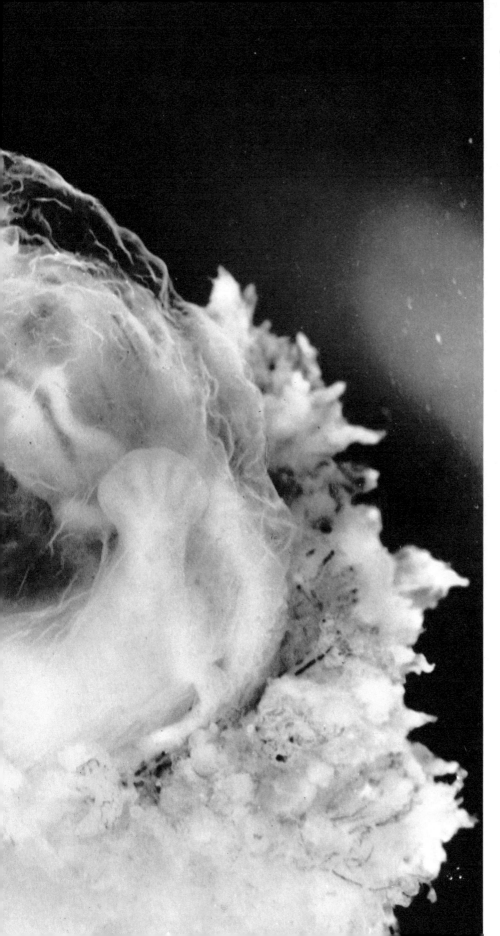

6 weeks,
½ inch

63

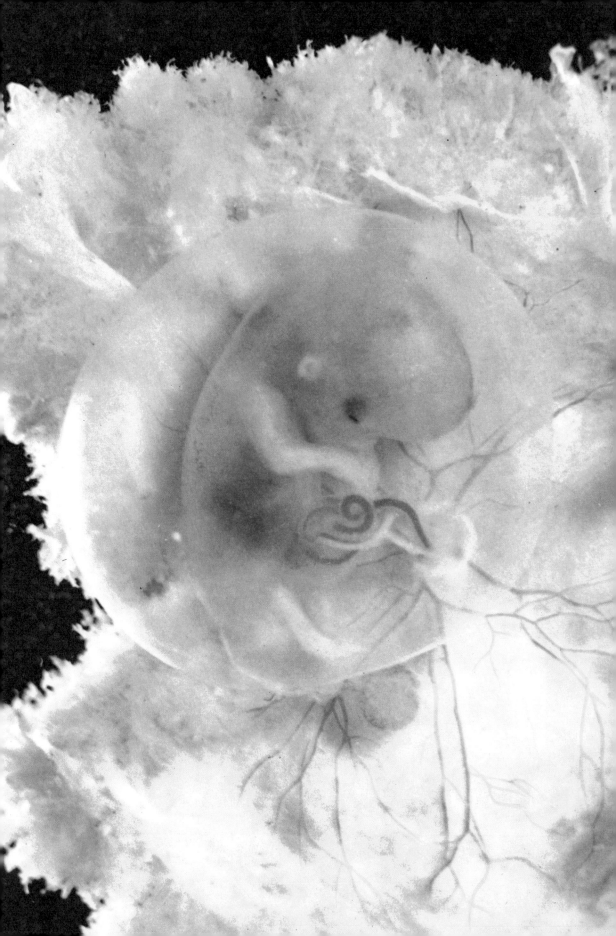

The baby is growing. With rapid beats the heart pumps the blood from its small circulatory system out into the immense tree of vessels in the placenta, where millions of villi absorb nourishment and oxygen for the little body. This baby is in the middle of its third month. The eyes are about to close; the ears are moving into proper position, and the arms and legs are approaching their final form. The yolk sac is losing contact with the circulation of the baby and hangs like a pale, anemic vesicle under the amnion.

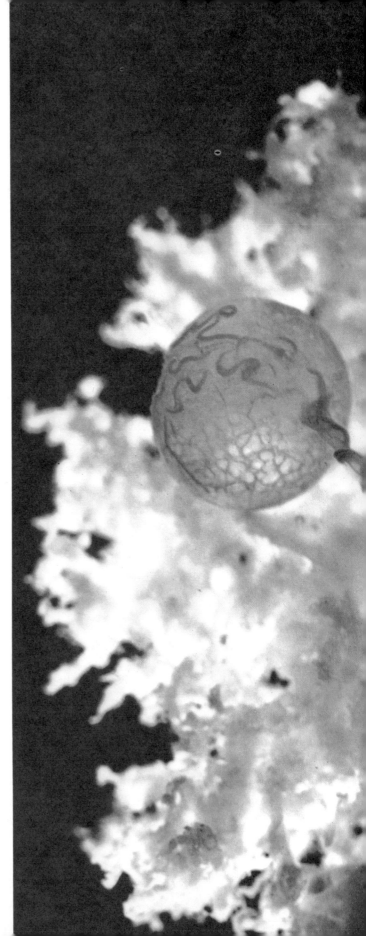

Nearly six weeks have passed since conception, and the menstrual bleeding will soon be four weeks overdue. In a couple of days the woman will know whether it will come this time or not. . . .

The baby, a plump little being over a half an inch long, with short arms and legs, floats in its amniotic sac, well moored by the umbilical cord. The large dark shadow in front is all the blood streaming through its liver and heart. Like a happy balloon the yolk sac sails fastened to its thin stalk; from it, fresh blood corpuscles are delivered to the circulation. The main part of the circulatory system is not within the body but out in the large placenta, where the blood is oxygenated and gets fresh nourishment and where carbon dioxide and waste products are filtered out.

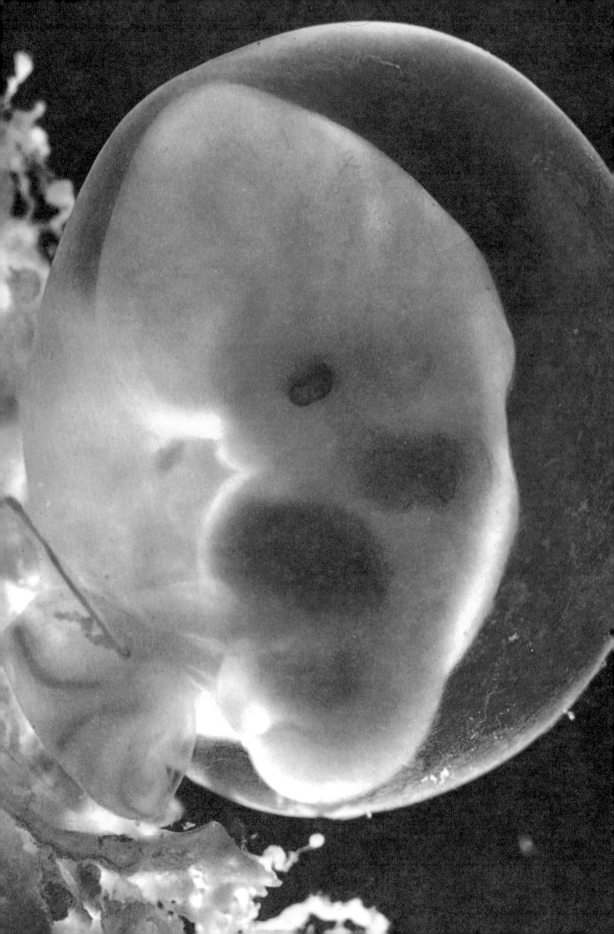

Here the baby is turning its back on us. It is not the head we see at the top but the neck. The head is bent forward with the chin on the breast and the trunk still does not comprise more than half of the body length. The skin is thin and translucent; we can see the shimmering spinal cord, and the vertebral arteries are the two delicately drawn lines on either side of it—the vertebrae are not fully developed until much later.

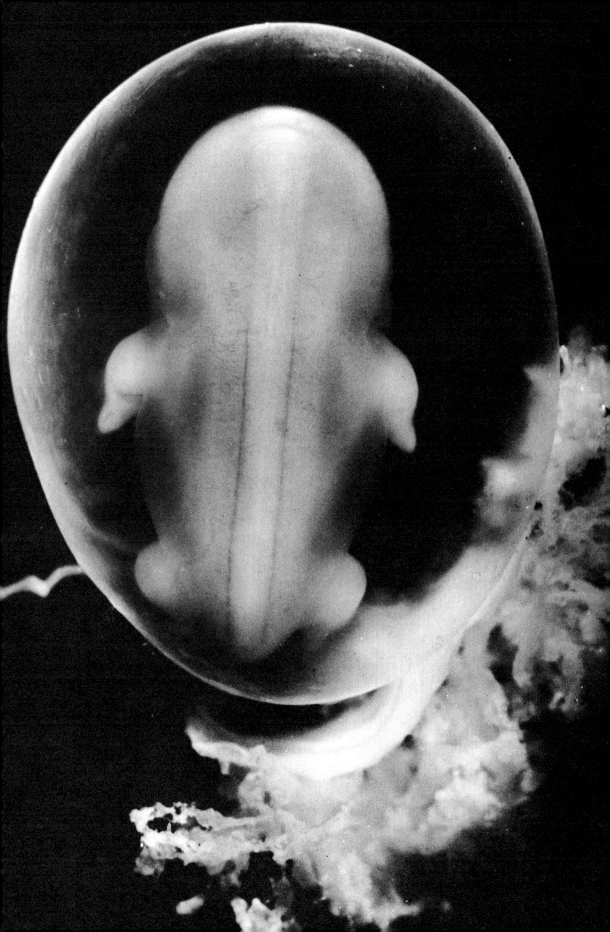

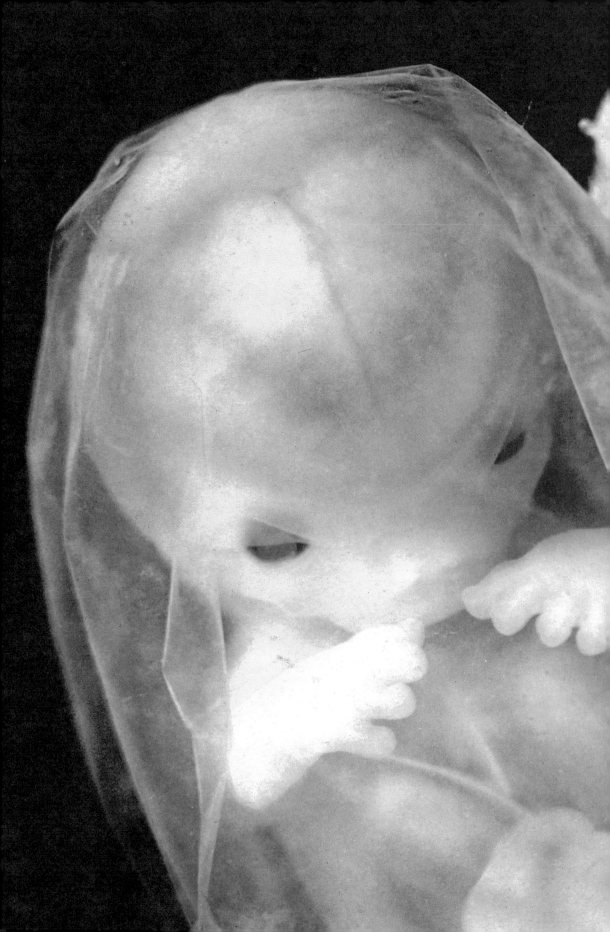

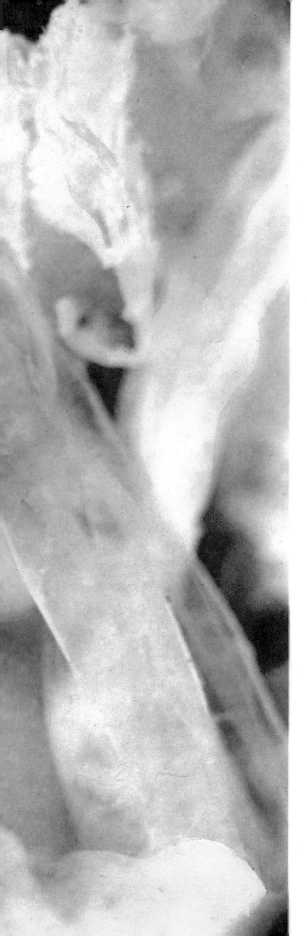

Eight weeks, over an inch. No longer an embryo but a fetus. From now on no further primordia will form; everything is present that will be found in the full-term baby. Now this human being must grow and all details must be perfected, all functions exercised. The heart has been beating for a month and the muscles have started their first exercises.

A human face with eyelids half closed as they are in someone who is about to fall asleep. Hands that will soon begin to grip, feet trying their first gentle kicks.

By now almost two and a half months have passed since the last menstruation. It has been missed twice. Time for the expectant mother to go and see the doctor: Is she going to have a baby, or . . . ?

71

First Visit to the Doctor

It is wise for a woman to pay a visit to her physician or to a maternity clinic once she has missed two menstrual periods. The doctor would like to see the patient he will be caring for relatively early in her pregnancy in order to determine the possibility of complications, either because of previous illnesses or in the pregnancy itself.

An experienced gynecologist can detect pregnancy by means of an internal examination approximately two weeks after the cessation of the menstrual period. The diagnosis is based on the fact that the mouth of the uterus has become soft and has taken on a bluish-red color. The uterus itself has also expanded, is rounder, and it too has become softer. In the case of a normal pregnancy there is usually no need for a pregnancy test.

In the early days of pregnancy the woman feels as though her menstrual period is about to start at any moment. There is a sense of heaviness in the lower abdomen because of the increased circulation of blood. Various pains may be felt in this region because of the expansion of the uterus. The breasts increase in size, and the tenderness usually felt in the breasts just before the menstrual period persists.

These symptoms are very indicative of pregnancy, but one cannot be totally certain without a medical examination. Filled with excitement, the woman makes an appointment. When she is shown into the doctor's office, he asks her to be seated and takes down her case history. First of all, age is important. If the mother is over thirty-five when she is carrying her first child, she is regarded as an older "primigravida," with perhaps a slightly greater tendency to complications in pregnancy and confinement, who must therefore be watched over more carefully. Having a first child before the age of twenty also seems to entail a greater risk of complications than during the ideal age span: between twenty and thirty.

Previous illnesses

The doctor will also gather information about previous illnesses and deliveries. Certain illnesses a woman has had earlier in life could possibly bring about complications in pregnancy. Among these are heart and kidney ailments. If they have been of a serious nature they can add to the risk of pregnancy, and the doctor will want to watch his patient with special care. A tubercular woman is certainly able to have children, but she too must be watched carefully during pregnancy. The doctor will also ask about venereal diseases. Gonorrhea does not complicate a pregnancy *per se*, but if the disease has not been treated, it can cause trouble after delivery and also injure the child. Possible consequences are genital infections and serious eye infections in the child.

Other questions: Does she have diabetes, or have either of her parents had it? A diabetic woman must be watched continually during her whole pregnancy. A woman with diabetes in her family—for instance, a diabetic mother—should take certain tests during pregnancy to ascertain whether or not she has a tendency toward diabetes.

After this the doctor will ask other questions. How old was she when she first menstruated? Are her periods regular? Has she ever been pregnant before? How many children has she had previously? What did they weigh? Were the deliveries long, or difficult? Did she, during any of the deliveries, bleed in excess of normal? Has there been any illness or anomaly in any of her previous children?

When will the baby be born?

The duration of pregnancy averages 280 days, calculated from the first day of the last menstrual period, and 95 per cent of all babies are born between the 266th and the 294th day. Deviations from this norm thus range, for the most part, up to fourteen days in either direction. Women with menstrual cycles of more than twenty-eight days often have a longer pregnancy. The accepted method of calculating the length of pregnancy is to establish the date of the first day of the last menstrual bleeding. To arrive at an estimated time of delivery, one adds seven days plus nine months. But this method is not completely accurate. Ovulation generally takes place fourteen days after the first day of menstruation, which means that during the first two weeks of the period under calculation, the woman is not actually pregnant. If the menstrual cycle is longer than twenty-eight days, the egg is also fertilized somewhat later. The estimated date of delivery is likely to be too early if the length of the menstrual cycle is not taken into account.

Miscarriages and other difficulties

A history both of previous miscarriages and of full-term pregnancies is important to the doctor in handling the present pregnancy. If the miscarriages occurred between the first and third months, they are usually regarded as inconsequential. As a rule these involve immature eggs with gross malformations. The body, fortunately, rids itself of such eggs. In the case of a miscarriage later in the pregnancy, a cause can often be found and perhaps eliminated in the present pregnancy. Big babies weighing over 10 pounds suggest a possibility of latent diabetes in the mother. Long-drawn-out deliveries can mean an undersized pelvic passage, etc. For all these reasons, a careful questioning of the mother-to-be is very important.

Examination

Following this, the doctor will proceed to the first examination. To begin with, it is necessary to take a sample of her urine, which will be tested for sugar and albumin content. After she undresses, her height is measured, and she is weighed. Then two samples of blood are taken from a vein in her arm (at the elbow joint). These are sent to special laboratories. One is a Wassermann test to determine the presence or absence of syphilis. The other is for the purpose of determining the mother's blood type (A, B, O, AB) and the possibility of the Rh factor (see "Third Visit to the Doctor"). A small sample is also taken for a blood count.

Then the mother lies down for her first examination. The doctor first does a complete general physical examination. Then he inserts into the vagina an instrument called a vaginal speculum which makes it possible for him to inspect the mouth of the uterus. As previously mentioned, this will be soft and bluish-red in color. With a small spatula and glass pipette he takes a cervical smear which will be sent out for cytological examination. By this means, any signs of cancer of the uterus can be detected. The doctor may also at this stage evaluate the pelvic bones to determine if there will be any mechanical difficulty from too small a pelvis.

In addition to the gynecological examination, the mother-to-be has her blood pressure taken and the doctor listens to her heart. The breasts are examined for lumps, which can be the sign of a malignant growth. The nipples are also examined.

In the beginning stages of pregnancy it is vital for a woman to get a well-fitted bra which will support and raise her breasts. They will soon become large and heavy, and if they are not properly supported, there is danger that the skin will stretch and the breasts will sag. The best treatment of sagging breasts is to prevent their sagging in the first place. At the end of the nursing period it is too late to do anything about it.

Finally the doctor examines the patient's legs to see if she has incipient varicose veins or if she has flat feet.

Advice for the beginning of pregnancy

The mother now gets dressed and returns to the doctor's office, where he will offer practical advice for the early stages of preg-

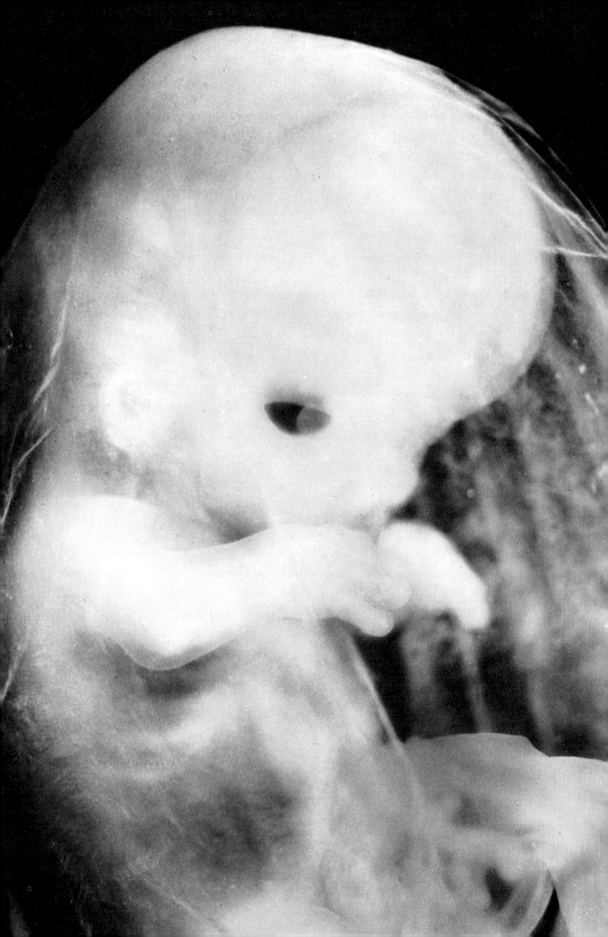

nancy. Pregnancy is a natural thing, but many extra demands are made on the body during this time. First, it must nourish a developing life and also cast off the waste products of the fetus. The whole body undergoes changes to help it fulfill this task. There is an increased need for nourishment, vitamins, and certain minerals and salts, which must be provided for. The increased production of hormones from the placenta breaks forth like spring floods; the mother's glands are stimulated to greater activity, and increased demands are made on all the organs. In the early stages this causes the mother to feel tired. She feels a need for more sleep, and to an extent she should give in to this need. As a rule, this need disappears later.

In the early stages there is often a tendency to slight nausea, and in some cases vomiting. In this event, it often helps to eat a breakfast of tea and toast in bed, and to stay in bed for a while. Meals should be small and frequent, but not amount to more than before pregnancy. If resting does not help, a change of scene can be very helpful.

Nowadays, medicines are prescribed for the expectant mother with caution. The Thalidomide tragedy made it clear that it is possible for drugs to hinder the development of the fetus. For this reason, the mother-to-be should not take any drugs which her doctor has not prescribed for her.

Increased need of iron

As far as possible, the mother-to-be should continue her normal life and her work. But because the fetus makes so many demands on her system, she will need certain supplements to her diet. For example, the fetus requires about one-third of the mother's supply of iron for the building of its own blood. This loss is not replenished after childbirth and the normal iron content of most diets is not sufficient to make up for the increased requirement. At the first visit, therefore, the doctor often writes out a prescription for iron capsules even if the mother shows no deficiency. To facilitate the absorption of iron, ascorbic acid is usually recommended. A pregnant woman may need extra vitamins—usually one all-purpose vitamin tablet per day is enough. The body also needs calcium. A pint of milk a day will usually provide enough for the pregnant

2 months, 1 1/5 inches

woman. If milk does not agree with her, cheese provides a good substitute.

What to eat?

It is completely unnecessary to "eat for two." A pregnant woman should not gain enormous amounts of weight. Obese women tend to have greater difficulties in conjunction with pregnancy. The normal weight gain should be about 20 pounds. The diet should provide a sufficient amount of protein. It should include meat, fish, eggs, fruit, and vegetables. Milk is important, either fresh or in the form of buttermilk or yogurt. Rolls and cake should be avoided. During pregnancy there is a great need for the B vitamins. Liver, whole-grain bread, egg yolks and brewer's yeast provide a good supply of these vitamins. If the mother suddenly has an irresistible desire for some special food, which she feels she must have at any cost, this is usually a sign of iron deficiency, and her iron consumption should be increased.

A dentist should be seen as soon as possible. During pregnancy small cavities in the teeth often become larger and must be cared for quickly.

Tobacco and alcohol

Many women ask about cigarettes and alcohol during pregnancy. Alcohol is safe in limited quantities; a glass or two of wine at dinner or a cocktail will do no harm. No one knows for sure whether or not tobacco is harmful to the fetus. It has been shown that women who smoke give birth to somewhat smaller babies. In making a decision about tobacco, the mother should also consider her own health and the increased danger, due to smoking, of lung and heart diseases.

Outdoor bathing

Swimming is perfectly healthy during pregnancy. Nowadays there are stylish, pretty bathing suits for expectant mothers. But at this time, the tendency to leg cramps is greater than usual. It is not a good idea to swim in very deep water or too far out from the shore. Sun bathing should be moderate. At times, because of pregnancy, unsightly moles will appear on the face, and too much sun will make these grow more unsightly and darker, and they will take a longer time to disappear.

Life as usual

The expectant mother should continue her normal life, including any sports she usually enjoys, but she should take it easier and not overexert herself. Travel, by any method, is perfectly safe for most women until the last month of pregnancy. A doctor will sometimes advise against travel if there is a history of premature labor or if he finds the cervix prematurely dilated. During the last months of pregnancy, it is wise to stay reasonably close to the hospital. Depending on the regulations of her employer, the pregnant woman should be able to continue working as long as she feels able.

The first visit to the doctor is over. Meanwhile, until the next visit, the expectant mother should watch her weight and general state of health. If anything unexpected occurs, she should call her doctor immediately.

For the mother-to-be now coming out of the doctor's office, the world suddenly seems full of pregnant women. It is like discovering that there is a different race of people mixed in with the rest, and that she herself now belongs to it.

But she does not feel as though she belongs to any part of this special race as yet. She does not look different, nor are her fellow mothers-to-be with their bulging figures likely to accept her as one of them. However, she is no longer her ordinary everyday self; she feels heavy, sometimes nauseated, notices that the taste and smell of things is different, is both happy and sad at the same time. Something has come over her. Nothing will ever be quite the same.

It is not surprising that she has difficulty in accepting herself as a mother during these first months. The baby is so small and somehow anonymous. In truth it does not yet look like anyone special, but resembles all other human fetuses of the same stage, just as it once resembled all other creatures which develop from sperm and ova. But it is already alive, a human being, although its movements are still too feeble to be felt. And it has immense power. It can make another person take care of it and adjust her whole organism to serve it.

When looking at a well-shaped, newborn baby one finds it quite fantastic that such a tiny being has fingers and toes, eyes, nose, mouth, and everything needed to make it complete. But we are apt to think that these things have been there all the time, that it all began one fine day with a miniature being of less than a millimeter, that grew and grew (unless we suppose it to be a shapeless, slimy mass till the day it quickens). At any rate, learned men of ancient times believed that a little homunculus sat crouched in every sperm head.

We have already seen that development does not take place like that. Now we shall dwell for a while upon details, to see how a hand, a foot, or a face emerge out of shapeless primordia. In all the figures the age is counted from conception. For the gestational age another two weeks are added.

2 months, 1 week
1½ inches

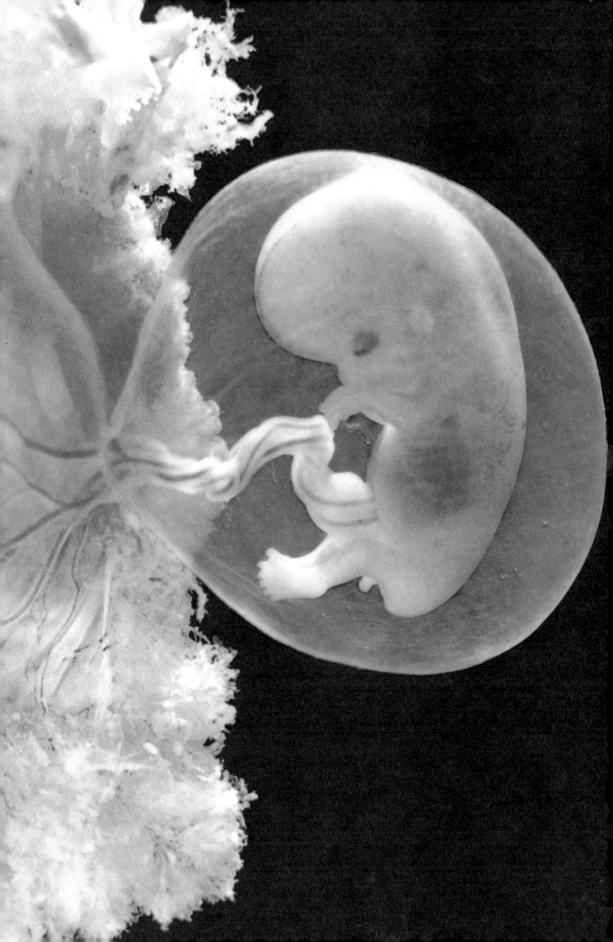

Girl or Boy?

The sex of the child is determined at the moment of conception. If a Y sperm reaches the ovum first, the new individual will have the combination XY in its chromosome set and will develop into a male. With an X sperm instead, the combination will be XX and a female child will result. As was described in the beginning of this book, it is possible to tell the sex from the chromosome charts obtained from single cells. If, for instance, the last pair is odd (X and Y), the cell derives from a male individual. As a rule, however, we are not looking for chromosomes when our babies are born. Fortunately there are much simpler ways to distinguish between boys and girls.

But during the first quarter of fetal development they look very much alike. The same sex gland and genital primordia are formed in both sexes. From then on, in normal development, sex chromosomes guide the differentiation of these primordia. In the beginning there is a slit with a swelling on either side and a small, rounded bud in between. In the female this stage prevails, the bud becomes a small, sensitive organ, the clitoris, and the swellings become the labia (majora and minora). In the male, development proceeds further. The bud grows into a penis that closes underneath around the urethra, and the swellings are fused to form the scrotum, into which the testes will descend later on. But even when the final form first begins to appear (as in the two small pictures) the resemblance is still striking.

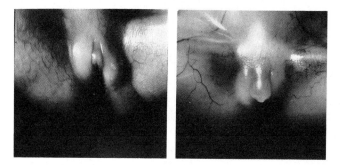

8 weeks, 1 inch

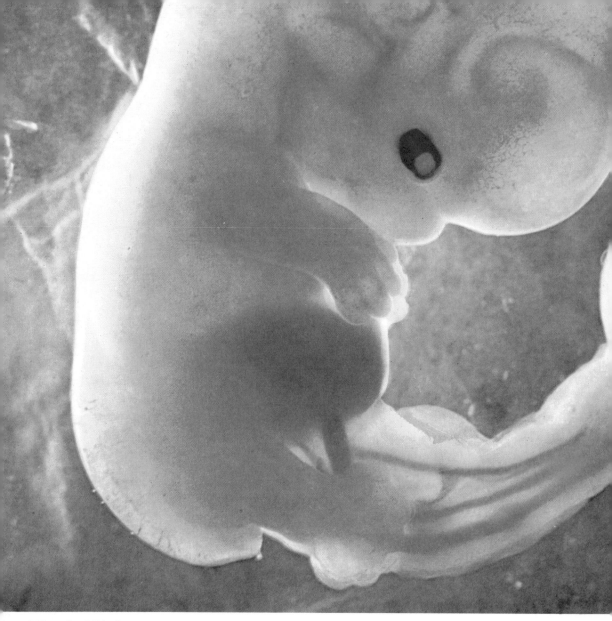

5½ weeks, 2/3 inch

6½ weeks   14 weeks   newborn

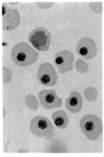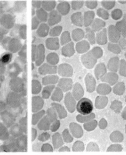

The red blood corpuscles (erythrocytes) transport oxygen. When mature they lack a cell nucleus. But in its early stages the growing organism cannot wait for them to mature and emits them into the blood with the nucleus still inside (left picture). The nucleated cells in the two pictures to the right are white blood cells.

Through the large umbilical vein the blood returns from the placenta with oxygen and nourishment. Before flowing back into the baby's circulation, it must pass through the liver (the large red shadow under the hand). At first it passes through all the small blood vessels in the liver tissue, but gradually a main duct forms for the bloodstream so that most of the blood can go from the umbilical cord rapidly to the heart and be pumped further.

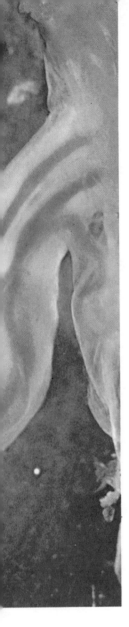

Until the third month, the baby has no bone marrow for the making of blood cells. They are first formed in the walls of the early blood vessels, especially in the ample network of the yolk sac wall. By the eleventh week, when the yolk sac has served its time and the stalk comes loose from its attachment, the liver and spleen have gradually taken over. During the third month they, in turn, will begin to be succeeded by the bone marrow of the growing skeleton. Up until birth, part of the blood cells will still be formed in the liver and spleen; later on the bone marrow will be the only source of the red and a majority of the white blood cells (the *leucocytes*).

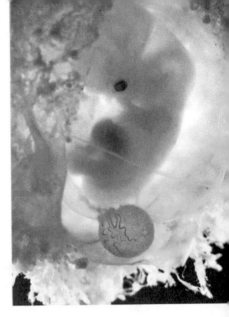

Just over 5½ weeks, ½ inch

The Blood

11 weeks, 2 inches

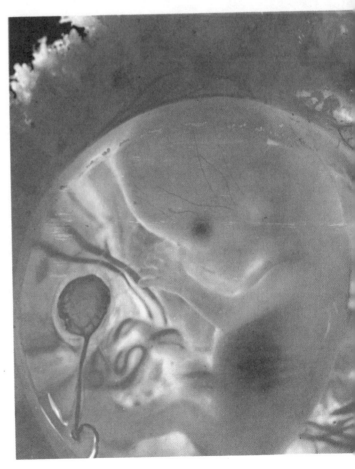

The *lymphocytes*, i.e., the white blood cells concerned with immunity, are formed by the so-called lymphatic tissue present in the lymph nodes, tonsils, spleen, thymus, and other parts of the body. The thymus is a glandlike organ behind the sternum in young individuals; it gradually degenerates after puberty. It is believed to play an essential role in the formation of lymphocytes and in immunological reactions during the fetal stage. In the eleventh week the thymus and lymph nodes are beginning to function.

11 weeks, 2 inches

Like an astronaut in his capsule the fetus floats in its amniotic sac with the villi of the placenta around it like a radiant wreath. The nebulae and constellations in this firmament are formed by cells from the maternal blood and salt crystals in the fetal waters.

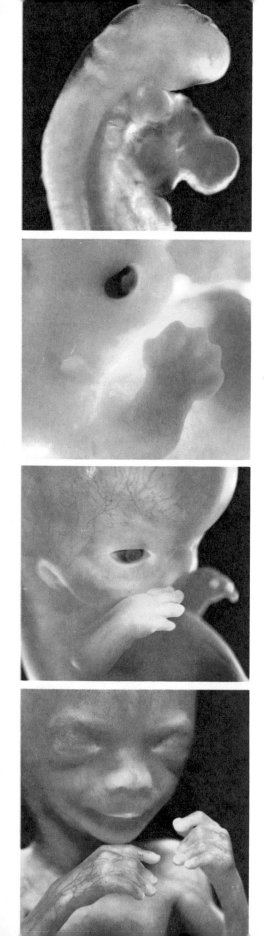

The Face

4 weeks, 1/5 inch. The face is only a forehead protruding above the future mouth. Three "neck" arches are seen behind the big heart. On the large picture of the same embryo (page 52), the developing eye primordium is also visible.

5½ weeks, 2/3 inch. The retina is dark because of the pigment in it. A lens has formed and in front of it a cornea. Just above the eye there is a faint indication of the developing eyelid. The ear is still placed rather low on the neck.

8 weeks, over 1 inch. There is now more of a face below the eyes, but the lower jaw is not yet fully developed. Thus the ears seem to be lower than they should. Now the lower parts of the face will grow rapidly, the baby's neck will stretch out, and the proportions will gradually become more "adult."

4 months, 6 inches. The chin is still tiny and the distance between the eyes seems too wide for such a narrow face. The eyes themselves seem a bit too big; the eyelids bulge under the brows. This is because the eyeballs are quite big from the beginning. Later the face will catch up.

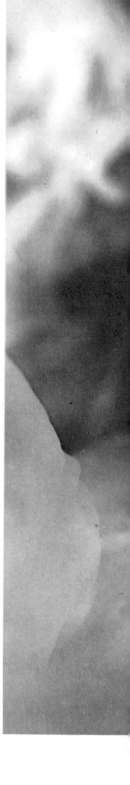

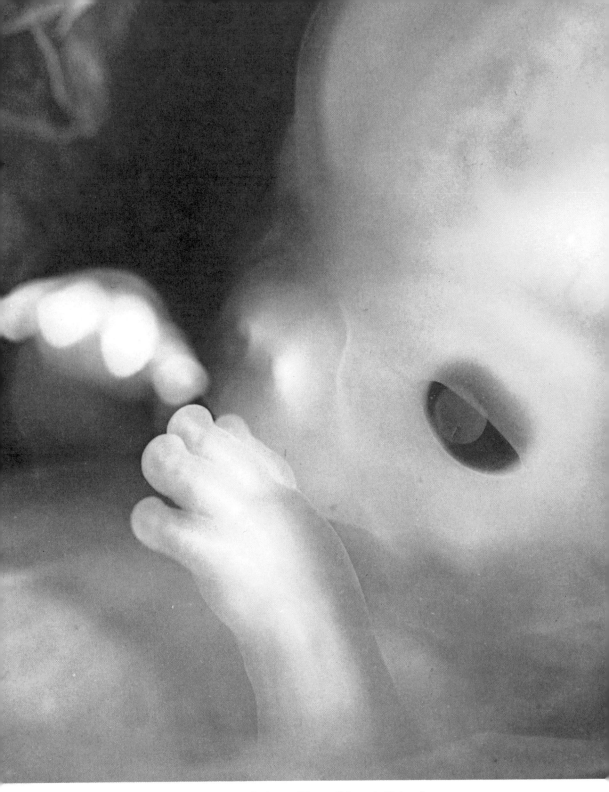

Portrait of the same baby as in the third small picture. The eyelids are half closed; in a couple of days they will close completely and remain so until the seventh month. The brain can be seen shimmering beneath the delicate skin. The body has no real skeleton yet.

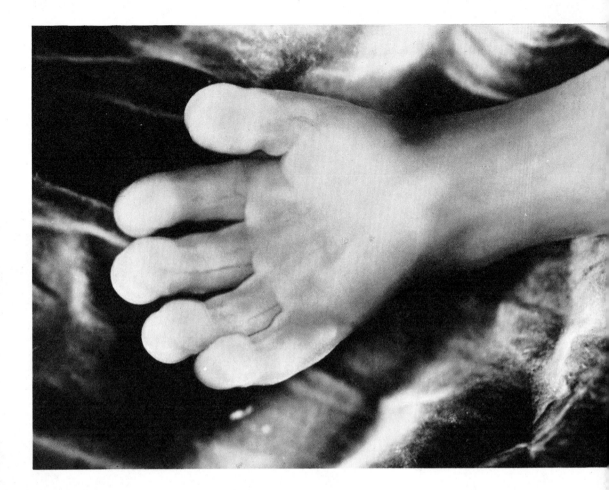

11 weeks, 2 inches. The eyes
are closed; the dark shadow
showing through is the pigment in the retina. Short,
clumsy fingers, on the tips of
which nailbeds are forming.
Weight: ¾ ounce, about the
same as a letter.

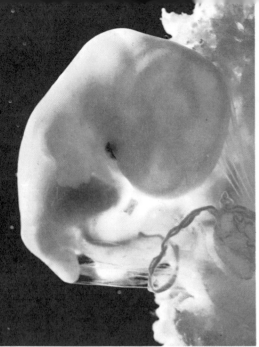

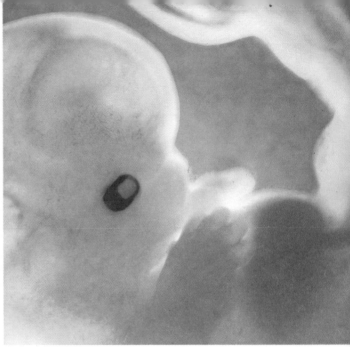

5 weeks, 2/5 inch. The hand is the part of the arm that grows most rapidly and appears first. The fingers are already seen budding, but there are no joints as yet.

5½ weeks, 3/5 inch. The end phalanx of the fingers has protruded beyond the "webs." The latter are still present in the adult as the rounded skin folds visible when the fingers are spread.

Hands

Lower left: 4½ months, 8 inches. The thumb is already a good thing, if not for consolation, for the assiduous sucking exercises that start as soon as the hand gets close to the mouth and the thumb slips into it. By now the arms and legs move vigorously when the baby is not asleep.

Lower right: 5½ months, nearly 12 inches. The nails are about to reach the fingertips (some children may scratch themselves thoroughly during the last weeks before birth). All the babies pictured have their arms flexed, the most comfortable position. During the whole prenatal development and for a short period after birth the flexor muscles prevail over the extensors. A healthy newborn may be held suspended by its bent arms for several minutes.

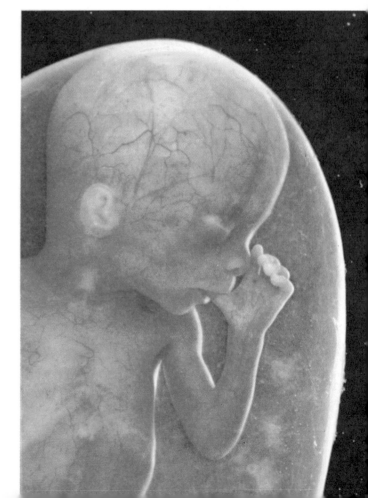

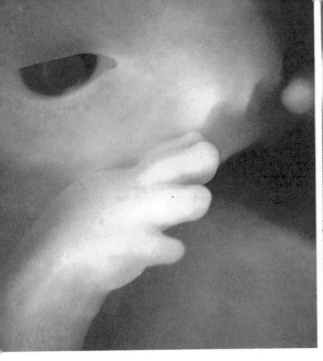

8 weeks, 1 inch. The arms have grown just long enough to enable the baby to touch its face, but they don't reach each other yet. Fingertips are forming.

4 months, 6 inches. Arms and hands are fully shaped. There are small, short nails on all fingers. The transparent cartilaginous skeleton is turning into bony tissue, starting in the middle of each skeletal bone and progressing toward the end.

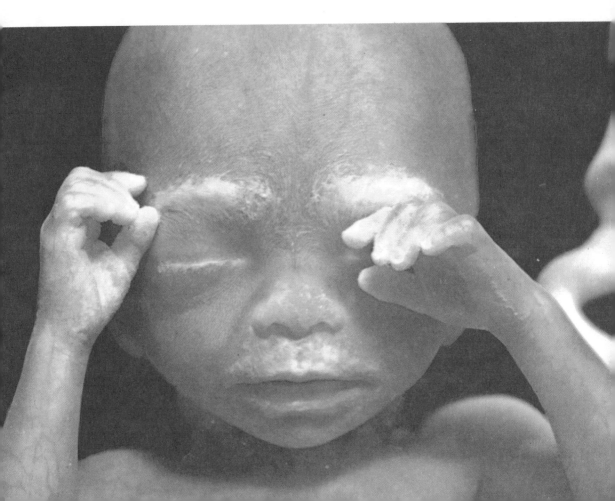

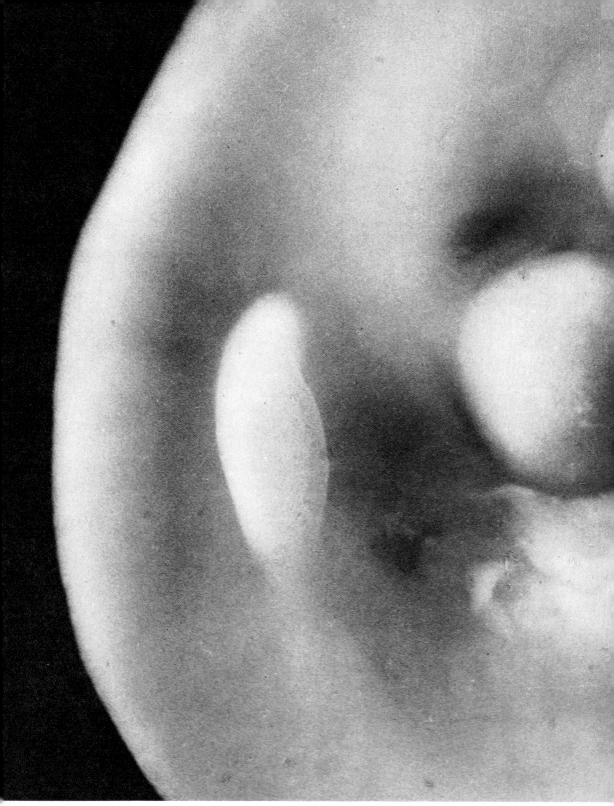

30 days

94

A precision tool—the hand—develops. It begins as a shapeless bulging on the side of the body, between the back and the spherical heart. But in the ground substance the way is prepared and the ultimate fate of every cell determined.

Almost 6 weeks

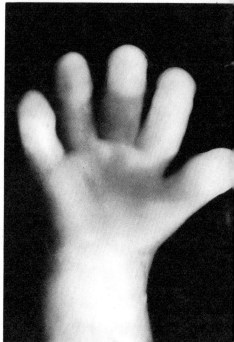

2 months 1 week

Almost 5 months

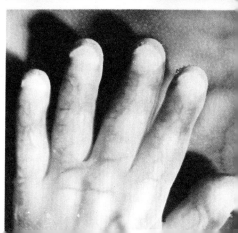

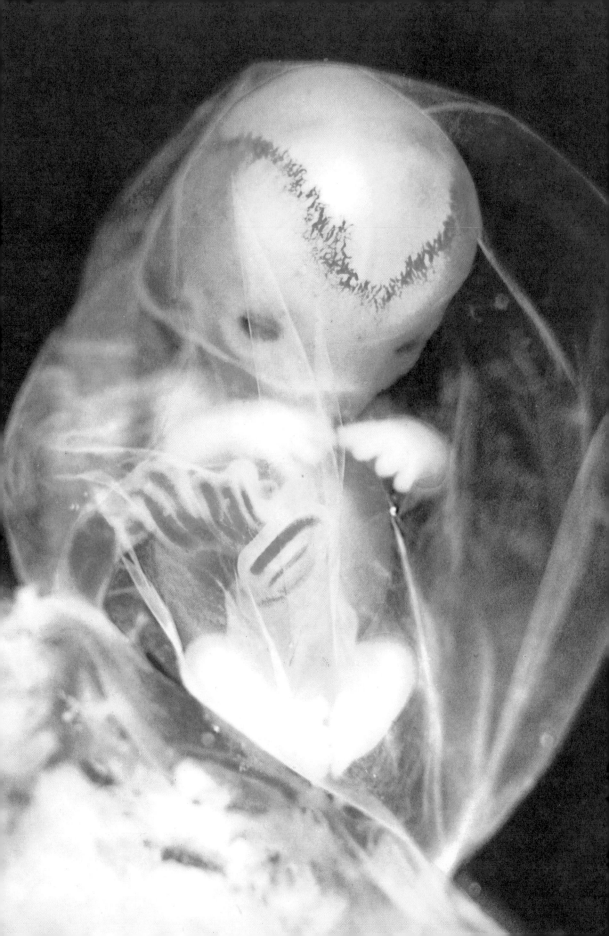

Just as the thin body wall is being strengthened by the outgrowth of muscles and connective tissue from the back, a better shelter is being prepared for the delicate brain than can be provided by the translucent skin. At the end of the seventh week a broad vascular border is seen moving toward the crown. Cerebral membranes are formed so that the brain will float in a shock-absorbing fluid bath. The subcutaneous tissue is also strengthened, and centers of bone formation appear at different sites at the base of the skull. From these centers the skull bones grow out in the form of thin plates beneath the skin, moving toward the crown. Like the petals of a flower cup they close protectingly around the developing brain.

But they must not fuse into an inflexible carapace. The head must be malleable not only in order to get through the narrow birth canal, but also to allow the brain to grow. At birth it has not yet reached its full size. The final fusion of the skull bones does not occur until just before puberty. At birth their edges can still glide along next to each other and are held together only by dense connective tissue.

The corners are rounded. Therefore, in the place where the skull bones meet, two boneless areas will be left: one large square above the forehead and one small triangle at the vertex, or crown (anterior and posterior fontanels). In the newborn, the anterior one is felt as a shallow, soft depression which gradually diminishes and disappears completely at the age of about eighteen months. Many parents are a little anxious when they discover that their babies have a hole in their heads and wonder whether there is any risk in touching the fontanel. The risk is actually negligible. The connective tissue that holds the skull bones together is as strong as first-class canvas.

97

Feet

5½ weeks, 3/5 inch. The foot is a rounded plate on which the buds of the future toes are scarcely indicated. The knee is still close to the trunk. The lower part of the trunk has not yet grown very much, so the umbilical cord ends almost between the legs.

4 months, 6 inches. The lower part of the body is still thin and slender, but now there is some belly below the cord as well. The feet and legs are fully molded. Within them the so-called ossification centers, i.e., those parts of the cartilaginous skeleton that have already been transformed into bony tissue, are seen as dark shadows. These centers grow toward the ends of the bones, but the cartilage grows, too. It is like a kind of chase, with the cartilage always a step ahead. Not until about twenty-five years of age does the last cartilage get tired and the chase come to an end. Then the bony skeleton is complete and growth ceases.

5 months, about 10 inches. The outlines are more rounded, suggesting the chubbiness of the newborn. This baby looks as if it were treading water, which is just what it is doing. The amniotic sac is still rather roomy, and at every vigorous kick the baby turns round and round, floating now head, now heels down.

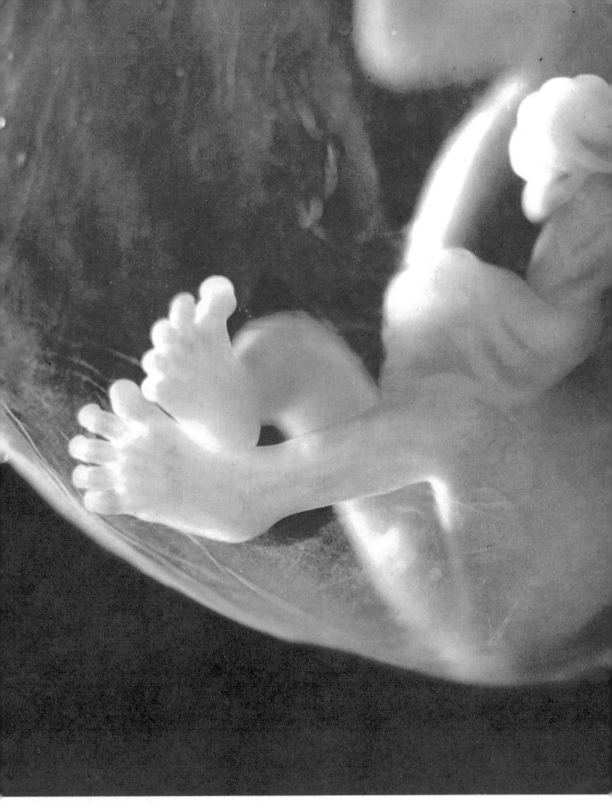

2 months, 1½ inches. The kicks from these tiny legs are still too weak to be felt; they will only stir up the fetal fluid.

In the beginning there was ample space. The embryo had plenty of room to turn over in the first chorionic cavity, when it was growing from a thin disk into a body with head and tail. Later the amniotic sac expanded and pressed outward, so that the uterine lining bulged and the uterine cavity was filled. Since then the whole uterus has grown, and the abdomen is swelling more and more. But pressing out the abdominal wall is not as easy as extending the thin amnion. The quarters will eventually become crowded. Earlier the fetus could lie and float about at anchor, as it were, kicking itself around without touching the walls. But now it bumps against them more and more every day. The mother feels this in sudden jerks and starts.

What was that the doctor said? "When I see you next the baby may have quickened."

Over 4 months, 8 inches

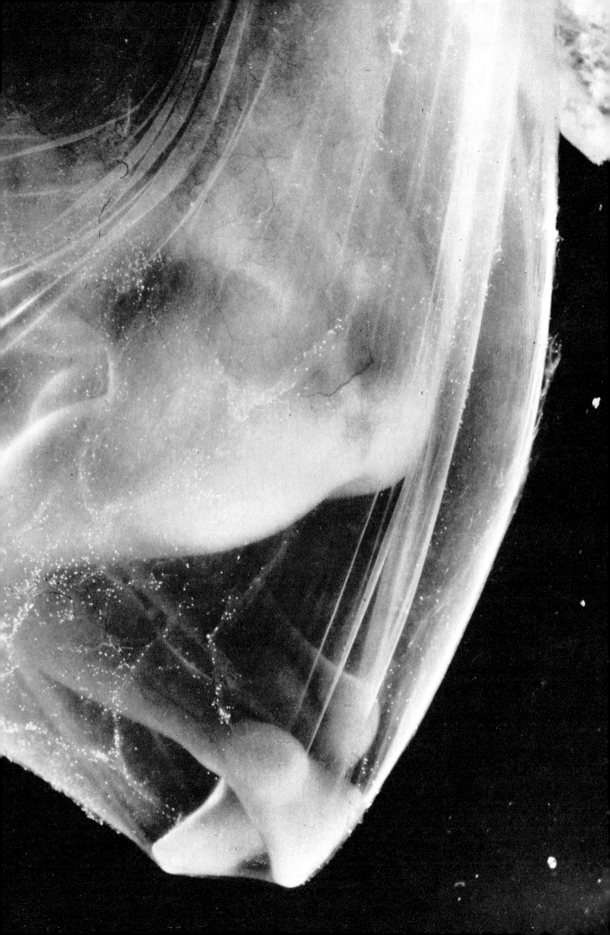

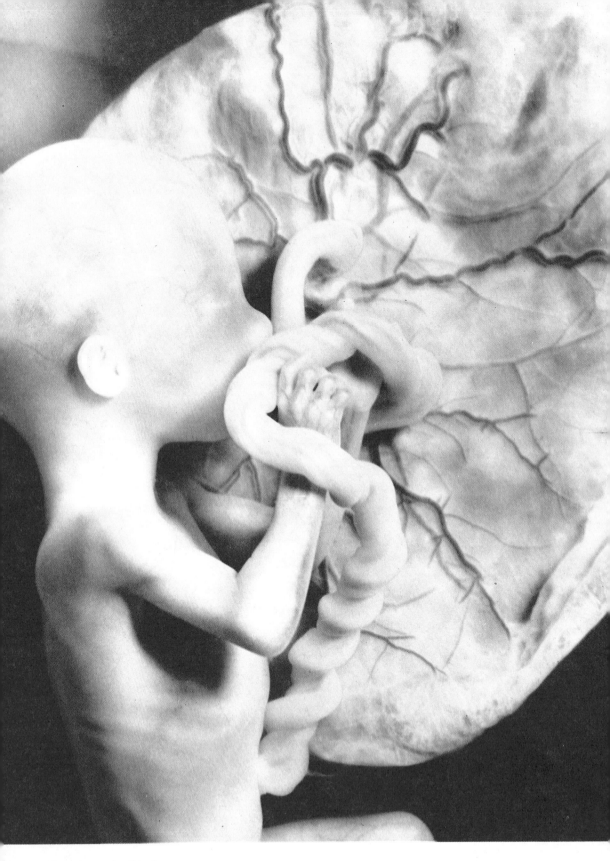

Over 4 months, 8 inches

Another Visit to the Doctor

Almost twenty weeks of pregnancy have passed. Something seems to be stirring in the lower part of the abdomen, which at first is hard to distinguish from intestinal rumblings—but which feels, as Sigrid Undset described it in *Kristin Lavransdatter*, like a kind of a fish tail. These are the movements of the fetus. A woman carrying her first child usually feels these stirrings in the twentieth week, but women who have had other children can feel them somewhat earlier. Actually the fetus has been in motion long before this, ever since the appearance of the embryonic arms and legs. In olden times it was said that the fetus "came to life" when the movements became sufficiently violent to be felt by the expectant mother.

The "stomach" is now rather round. The expectant mother is the object of certain knowing glances. Aha, so she's pregnant. She must let out her skirt a little around the waist and start to wear a maternity smock.

The doctor has fewer questions to ask this time, and more to observe. He wants to see if the expectant mother looks fatigued, if her face is bloated, and if her hair has lost its sheen—all signs of strain. Her urine is once again examined for albumin and sugar. She is weighed, for her weight tells all too clearly if rolls and cake have been abundant in her diet.

Examination of the uterus

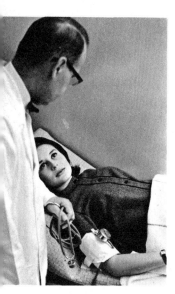

The expectant mother again lies down on the gynecological examination table. During this part of pregnancy there are increased secretions from the uterine passage and the vagina, which may alarm her. There is nothing dangerous about this; it is totally natural. At times, however, an irritation appears, caused by an ordinary fungus called *monilia*. In this event treatment is necessary.

The doctor may examine the cervix to see if it is properly closed. In certain cases it may prove to be too weak to withstand the pressure exerted upon it by the developing fetus and may begin to open too early. The dangers of premature birth accompanying this condition can be prevented by constructing a "cerclage," i.e., the passage is sewed together with a special sort of suture.

Following this examination, the mother will rest for a while before her blood pressure is taken. If this has risen since the first visit, it constitutes a danger signal.

The expansion of the uterus is noted. By now it should have reached the height of the navel, and the fetal heartbeat can be heard with a stethoscope. Often a mother wonders if she is expecting twins. After five months or more it is usually possible to determine this without X rays. There is a certain possibility of twins if the uterus is larger than it should be at this juncture and if it is abnormally wide. However, the mother-to-be should not become apprehensive if her doctor feels there is good reason for a diagnostic X ray. Though all exposure to radiation carries certain risks, the amount received in a single X ray is very small, approximately one twentieth of the cumulative dose considered safe before the age of thirty. It is wise to avoid "routine" X rays and those which are not necessary for the conduct of labor or pregnancy.

Varicose veins

Once again the doctor examines the patient's legs to see if any varicose veins have broken out. If they are present, the usual procedure is to wait until a few months after delivery before treating them, to give them a chance to disappear by themselves. During pregnancy the mother should wear support stockings at the first sign of varicose veins. Such support helps prevent the veins from enlarging and allows the blood to circulate more easily. The stockings ought to be put on before getting up in the morning. Beforehand the legs should be massaged in an upward direction to decrease the swelling. The stockings can be rolled down to the foot portion and then put on.

Blood count

Again the patient's blood count is taken, which immediately shows if anemia is present. In this event she will probably feel fatigued. If the mother-to-be has been taking iron capsules, the doctor will look further for the cause of this deficiency. In certain cases it can happen that the mother is allergic to ordinary iron capsules and experiences diarrhea or constipation. Injections of iron may be necessary in order to sustain the proper level.

Hemorrhoids

By the time the fetus approaches the twentieth week any nausea experienced in the early stages has usually disappeared. Feelings of depression and discouragement—if there have been any—are also gone, and in general women at this stage look forward with growing confidence and happiness to the time of delivery. But the expectant mother often wants to ask the doctor about certain lesser discomforts. There may be hemorrhoids—varicose veins, so to speak, in the rectal opening. As the expanding uterus presses downward, the backflow from the blood vessels in the placenta is hindered, and if there is also constipation, discomfort sets in easily. The remedy for this is exercise, drinking plenty of water, and perhaps a laxative. In addition, the doctor can prescribe a healing, soothing salve or some appropriate suppositories.

Cramps and heartburn

A pregnant woman may experience painful cramps in the calves of her legs, her thighs, and her toes. The cramps generally appear at night. They are of unknown cause. They are sometimes relieved by large doses of thiamine, one of the B vitamins. Heartburn is another ailment which often appears in mid-pregnancy. The expanding uterus forces the stomach cavity out of its usual position, and gastric juices are pushed up into the esophagus. There are good medicinal aids for this discomfort.

Maternity girdle

At this time, in mid-pregnancy, there is much to be discussed. The normal routine, urged in the early days, should now be somewhat restricted. A woman who has had children previously often needs to get a maternity girdle to support the weight of her expanding abdomen. The abdomen should be supported from below, and there should be a separate garter belt. The woman pregnant for the first time generally doesn't need a maternity girdle.

Gymnastic exercises

In order to strengthen the back and the abdominal muscles, and to attain that extra feeling of well-being, gymnastic exercises during pregnancy are very helpful. Such courses, attended by many mothers-to-be in Sweden, are not widely available in the United States. The expectant mother might wish to ask whether anything similar is offered in her community. No one should be lured into thinking, however, that gymnastic exercises will in themselves ensure a painless delivery. This is only one of several procedures employed to facilitate delivery and make it as painless as possible.

Especially important is an exercise to prevent the muscles of the pelvic floor from becoming weakened. This is the so-called pinching exercise, which can be practiced at home. With the sphincter muscles, the mother-to-be pinches as hard as she can, as if she were trying to keep from urinating. This should be done time and time again, daily. Nothing is better for preventing a prolapse, or difficulty in controlling urination following delivery.

In connection with the future delivery it is vital that the woman

Sit tailor fashion, alternately placing one hand on the head and the other straight out to one side. At the same time rotate the head.

Stand on the outsides of the feet with toes turned inward. Curl the toes.

Lie on the back with the arms flat on the floor along the sides. Bicycle.

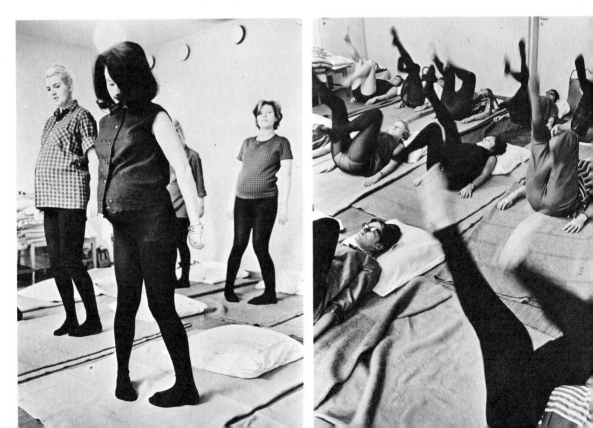

Left. Sit tailor fashion. Clasp elbows. Rock vigorously back and forth.

Lie on the back with the arms along the sides, bend knees, keeping feet on the floor. Raise hips.

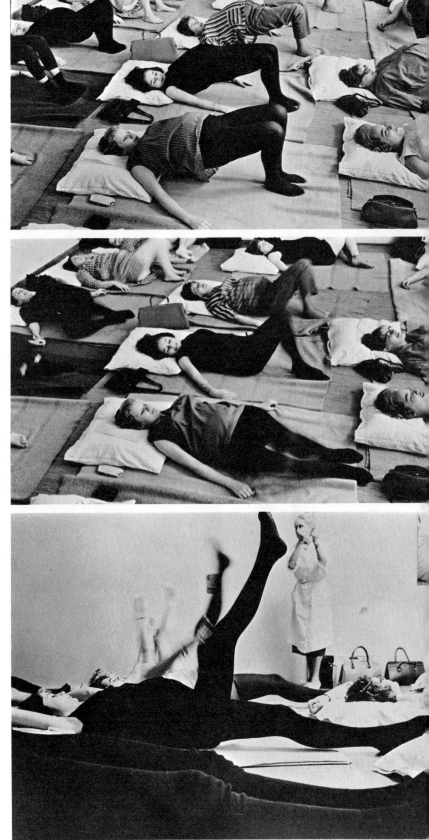

Flat on the back with knees bent: a) contract stomach, tense buttocks muscles, press back flat against the floor; b) relax and sway from side to side.

Flat on the back, with arms straight up. Raise one leg and then the other, placing hands on the knees.

Scissor motions with the arms held straight out in front.

Flat on the back with knees bent. Relax. Breathe with abdomen. Be sure abdomen moves.

learn to relax. Such training can make it much easier to endure the strain of labor pains. Worry about pain during delivery causes some women to tighten up unconsciously, and this tenseness often heightens perception of pain. It is important for the woman to relax completely between pains so that she may rest and not become so fatigued. A tired person is much more susceptible to pain than a rested one.

During the delivery the mother should know how to breathe with her diaphragm in order to ease the birth process. For this reason abdominal breathing is often taught in prenatal classes. Gymnastic exercises also help lessen the difficulties that accompany increasing weight. In order to balance the new weight in the front, the back must work harder, causing a greater strain on the muscles. Certain exercises can counteract this strain, including one where the mother-to-be is on all fours and alternately raises and sways her back.

Toxemia

Toxemia is the commonest of the complications arising during pregnancy. The symptoms are swelling of the hands, feet, and face, a gain in weight, the appearance of albumin in the urine, and a rise in blood pressure. In severe cases convulsions can occur, a condition equally dangerous to mother and child. Preventive health care appreciably lessens the chance of such complications. The better a country's system of prenatal care and health control is, the fewer the chances of toxemia in pregnancy. An expectant mother and her doctor should be on the watch for three things: bodily swelling, albumin, and a rise in blood pressure. The appearance of any of these symptoms is a warning signal. Rest and the restriction of salt and other sources of sodium are important in the treatment of toxemia. Modern-day living is filled with demands upon a pregnant woman because of the double job which she must accomplish. More rest, a change in diet, possibly even a short stay in a hospital, or additional help at home can cause the symptoms, in many cases, to disappear.

Weight gain and albumin

As far as weight is concerned, the mother, as a rule, should not gain more than 20 to 25 pounds during the entire term of pregnancy. If she gains too much weight, she should see her doctor more regularly. It is well to have a bathroom scale for the purpose of watching one's weight. Often increased weight is due not so much to swelling as it is to caloric intake, which should be watched. One way to distinguish between a weight gain due to swelling and one due to overeating is to take off one's wedding ring. If this is difficult, it is pretty certainly a sign of an unnaturally high concentration of water in the tissues. In this event, the expectant mother should contact the maternity clinic or her doctor.

Albumin in the urine is also a warning symptom. At most maternity clinics there are regular checkups which include blood pressure, urine, and weight. A private doctor will perform these tests at each prenatal visit.

Hygiene

Personal hygiene should be meticulous during pregnancy. Increased metabolism often causes a woman to feel abnormally warm and to perspire much more than usual. It is not harmful to take a bath, as many people believe; on the contrary, a daily bath is recommended. An increase in vaginal discharges means that this area must be carefully washed morning and night and after each visit to the toilet. Strangely enough, some women have the idea that soap and water are harmful to one's genitals. Nonsense. The mother-to-be should wash herself carefully, rinse away the soap, dry the area with a soft towel, and, if desired, apply a little talcum powder.

From the middle of pregnancy on, the nipples should receive special care. The breasts are now producing liquid which seeps out and which, when it dries, causes scabs. The nipples should be properly washed with soap and lukewarm water, after which an oily salve should be applied to keep them pliable. In the case of inverted nipples, massage may restore them to normal.

Sexual relations

What happens to sexual relations? How long may intercourse be continued? Many women are unhappy because they lose their desire for sexual relations during pregnancy. Women with a tendency for miscarriages might be wise to cease intercourse at the times when their menstrual period would normally occur if they were not pregnant. Otherwise, sexual relations may continue as long as the woman desires. However, it must be pointed out that personal hygiene on the part of both partners must be especially meticulous. Some doctors feel that intercourse too close to delivery time is risky and can cause infection, especially if either partner is at all lax in matters of personal hygiene.

Clothing

Finally, there is one matter which should be discussed, and that is what the mother should wear from the time it is obvious she is pregnant up to the time of delivery. As far as shoes are concerned, very high heels are not recommended since they cause too much of a strain on the back. Heels should be under two inches. At home any comfortable shoes will do, except slippers without heels.

There is the matter of underclothing. We have already mentioned the bra. An ordinary panty girdle will usually give enough abdominal support to a woman carrying her first or second child. A woman who has had many children may need a maternity girdle.

Because the pregnant woman often feels warm, lighter clothing may be appropriate. Cotton or lightweight wool is good. There are styles especially created to hide the expanding stomach. The mother-to-be will want to pay extra attention to her appearance, wash her hair often, take care of her hands, and wear nice accessories.

That is all for now. The expectant mother returns happily to her job and household, and to waiting.

It is perhaps not very easy to think "our baby" about an anonymous
little being of less than eight inches. It still lies floating in enough
fetal fluid within the amniotic sac so that its mother scarcely feels
if it gives a start sometimes. But still, the very notion of a new life
down there in the womb makes the pregnancy feel like something
more than just a strange sickness or a series of changes in the body.
The world is no longer full of other pregnant women. Somehow
it seems full of children.

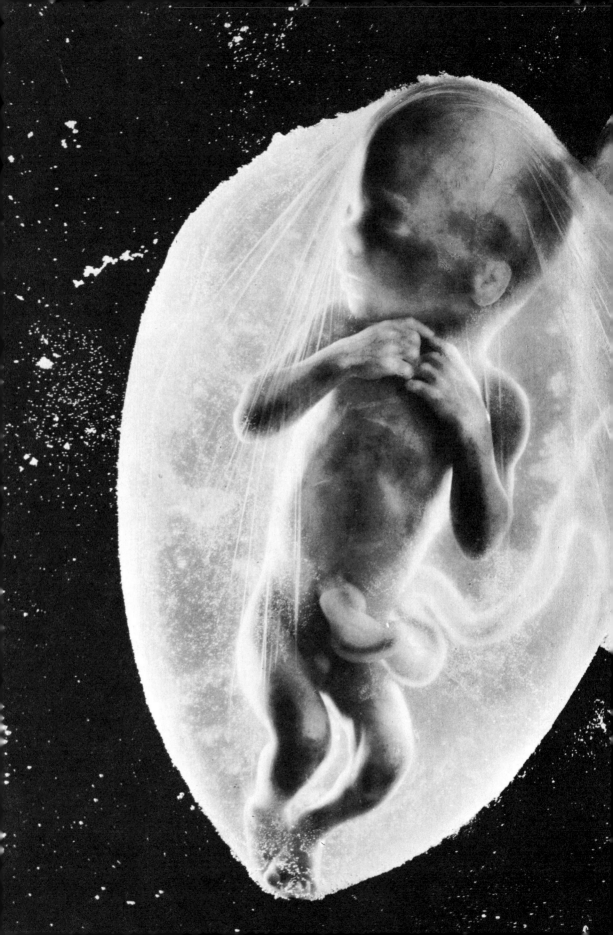

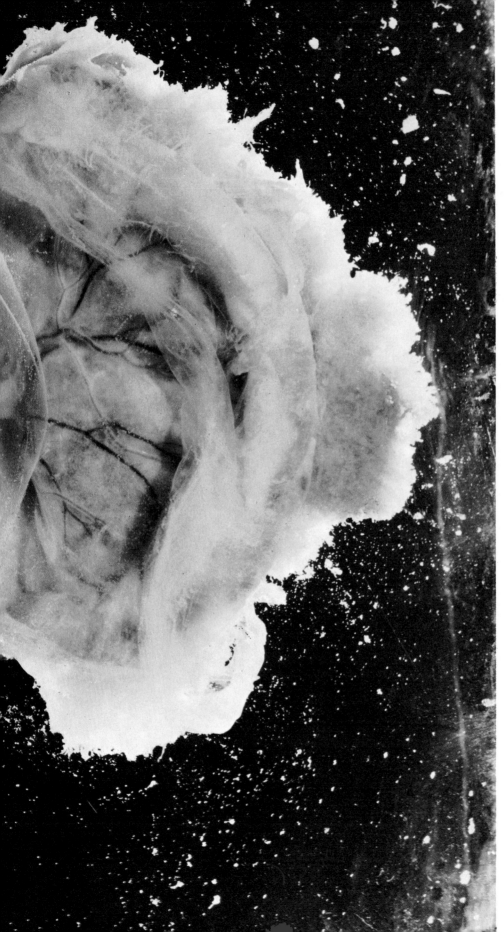

Over 4 months
8 inches

Over 4 months, 8 inches

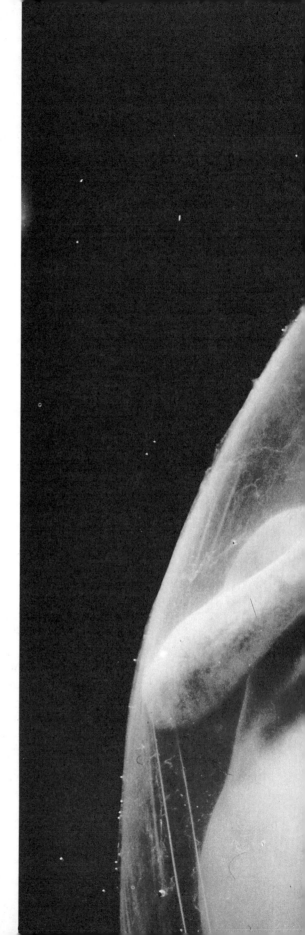

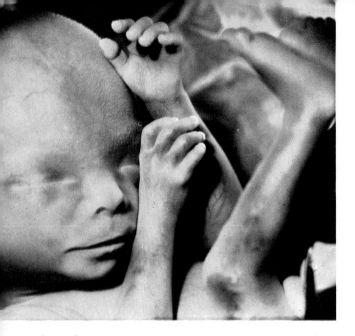

4 months
6 to 6½ inches

5 months
10 inches

Closed Eyes

There is an unearthly calm in these faces. They look as though they were awaiting eternity. But they are preparing for a short life on earth, and it is not sleep that closes their eyes.

When the eyelids meet in the beginning of the third month, the cells at their edges fuse. The lids are glued together, so to speak, and the eyeballs, which have not yet passed through the most critical stage of their development into functioning visual organs, lie well protected. Human babies will open their eyes again well before birth. But everyone who has seen newborn kittens knows that several days go by before they can look at the new world with their clear-blue eyes.

The skin is beginning to be fully developed. The first downy hairs are seen, especially at the eyebrows and on the crown. But blood vessels still shine through the translucent surface.

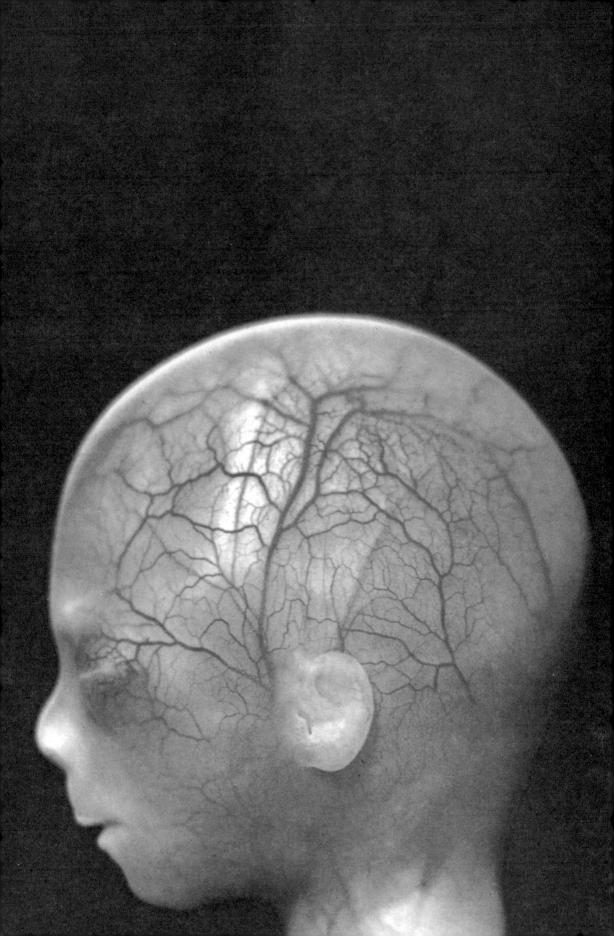

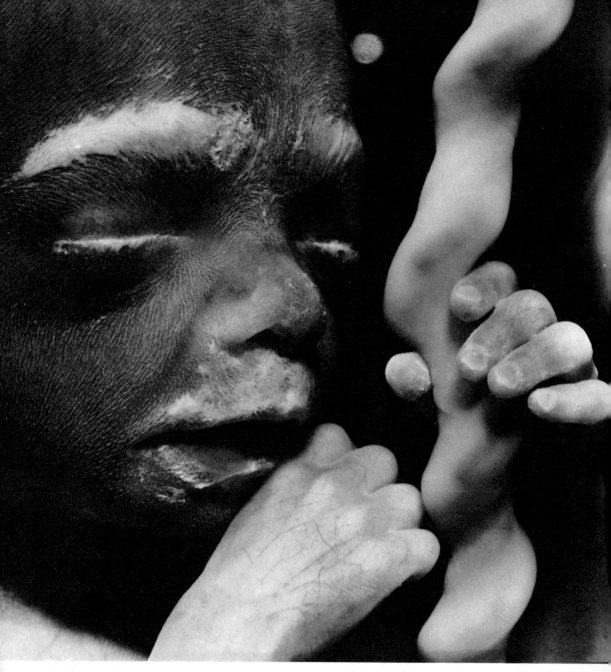

5½ months, 12 inches

The Umbilical Cord

The baby grips its cord, which can take vigorous squeezing. The two arteries and the vein passing through it are embedded in a firm, gelatinous substance. The pressure of the onrushing bloodstream keeps the envelope of the cord—part of the amnion—extended so that it will never kink or knot, no matter how much the baby turns around during its swimming exercises.

The coiling of the vessels is due to the fact that they grow faster than the cord itself. Thus there will be no risk of overstretching them. The length of the cord will also allow the child to move as freely as the space permits. At birth it is usually at least as long as the child, i.e., about 20 inches.

5 months, over 10 inches

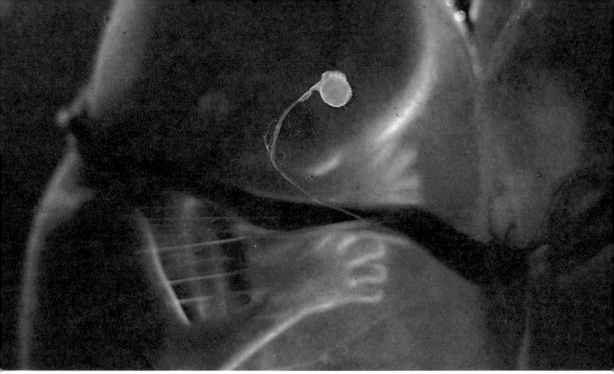

4 months, 6 inches

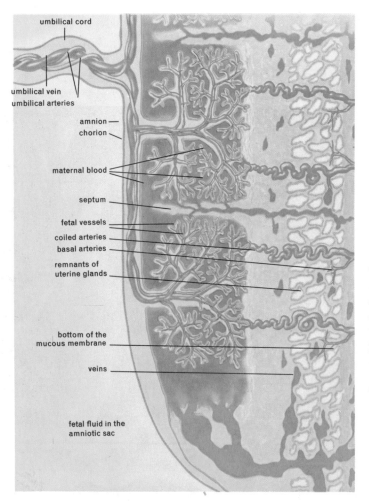

umbilical cord

umbilical vein
umbilical arteries

amnion
chorion

maternal blood

septum

fetal vessels
coiled arteries
basal arteries

remnants of
uterine glands

bottom of the
mucous membrane

veins

fetal fluid in the
amniotic sac

The yolk sac in the upper picture is but a memory of what it was at the time when the baby was not yet self-sufficient in its production of blood corpuscles. It will never grow larger than 1/5 inch across. Now a small, slack vesicle, it lies jammed between the amnion and the chorion. This baby now has a functioning bone marrow and also gets blood cells from its liver and spleen.

The schematic figure to the left is an attempt to present the structure of the placenta at work. The direct observation of this is, for obvious reasons, impossible. Therefore, all pictures can only be reconstructions, and opinions differ as to the real appearance. What cannot be shown in a still picture is, for instance, how contractions in the uterine wall compress the different compartments so that the maternal blood spouts past the villi with fresh oxygen and nourishment. The placenta has been called the "external heart of the fetus."

The Placenta—Mediator of Nourishment and Protective Barrier

The full-term placenta is as large as an ordinary soup plate. It weighs about 1 pound, 2 ounces and contains nearly 100 cubic centimeters of the fetal blood. It is shaped like a large basin with several partitions, covered by the chorion and amnion and with its villi suspended like dense branches toward the bottom, where the lowermost ones are firmly anchored. The basin is filled with maternal blood from the arteries of the uterine mucous membrane and is emptied through the large veins.

The fetal blood is pumped through the umbilical arteries out into the villi of the placenta. There only a thin cell layer separates the maternal from the fetal blood. Through this layer carbon dioxide streams out and is replaced by oxygen; waste products are released and nourishment brought in. The cell layer is also a barrier against many noxious agents and infections.

At the tips of the villi the maternal blood is rich in oxygen and nourishment, having just been pumped in from the uterine arteries. There the fetal blood turns and starts on its way back to the cord.

From the superficial cells of the villi, estrogens and progesterone are secreted from the second month of pregnancy until the end. These hormones are released into the maternal blood to keep the pituitary silent and to take over from the corpus luteum, which is unable to provide hormones for more than a month or so after the missed period. Thus during the main part of pregnancy the baby does not depend upon the hormones of the mother to be able to stay in the womb. But toward term the fine balance is gradually upset; the uterine musculature is no longer inhibited by the placental hormones and finally the mechanism of childbirth is unleashed.

Thus the placenta is many things at the same time: lungs, digestive organs, kidneys, attachment and protective barrier for the baby, as well as a potent hormone gland for the mother—an ingenious mechanism which is discarded at the very height of its activity.

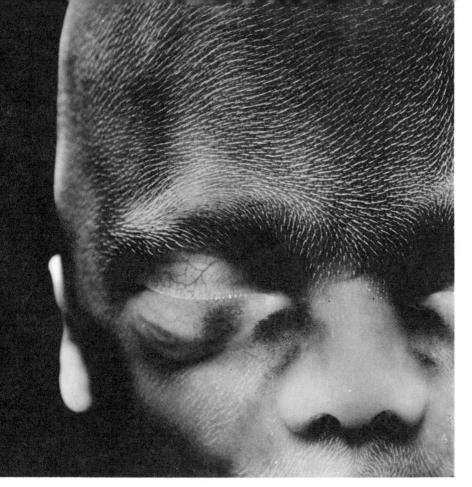

4½ months, 10 inches

Hair

The first hair appears as early as the beginning of the third month. This is a kind of vibrissae or whiskers on the upper lip, the eyebrows, and—curiously enough—on the palms and soles. Gradually these coarse primordia disappear and a softer hair, called the lanugo, develops all over the body like a downy fell. The hair follicles lie obliquely, parallel to the traction of the fibrous connective tissue in the true skin, or the corium. A linear pattern results, with whorls and curves like a fingerprint. In the fourth month the eyebrows and the hair of the head become more marked as coarser terminal hairs begin to grow. In those babies having a hereditary disposition for dark hair, the pigment cells of the hair follicles start making black pigment.

Nearly all the lanugo hair is shed before birth. The hair of the head, eyebrows, and eyelashes grows rather slowly; the coiffure at this early stage looks nicely trimmed.

126

5½ months, 12 inches

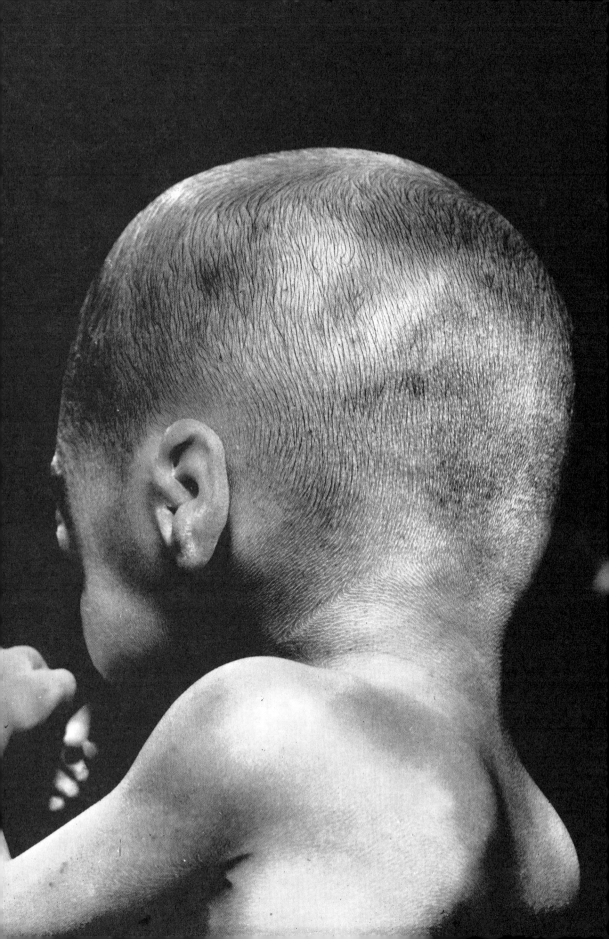

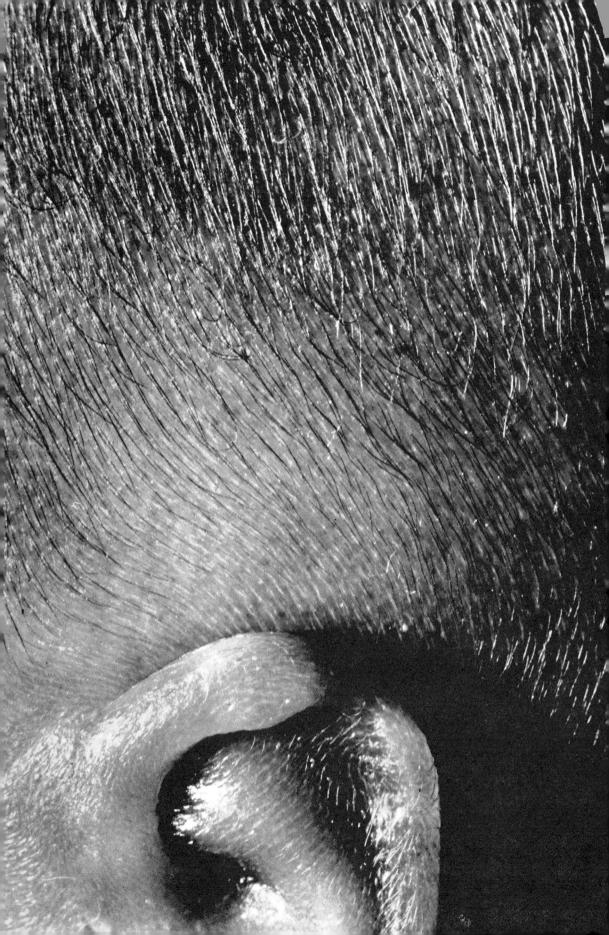

On the lanugo-haired border of
the ear one can see the notch
that was once pointed out by
Darwin as proof of our descent
from animals with pointed ears.
Above the ear the thin lanugo
hairs are gradually covered by the
coarser and darker terminal hairs
which will form the first wispy,
or shaggy, tuft on the baby's
crown.

4 months

The thin lanugo hair follows the
same pattern on the skin as does
the hair on the head: the upper
whorl is from the forehead, the
lower one is the vortex which
determines in which direction the
mother will brush the baby's hair.

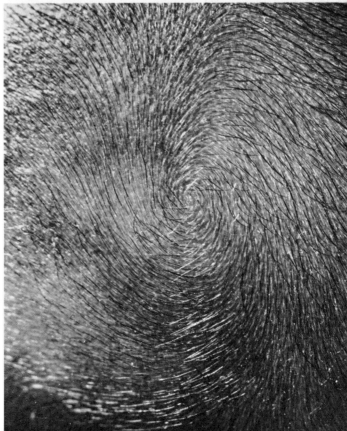

5½ months

5½ months, 12 inches

The Protective Ointment

Next to each hair are one or more sebaceous glands which provide an oily substance called sebum to keep the hair lustrous and the skin soft. This is especially important during pregnancy, when the baby floats in water. The skin must not become sodden. The sebum from the sebaceous glands and cells shed from the epidermis form a protective ointment, called *vernix caseosa*. The lanugo hairs help the vernix cling to the surface of the skin. Hence, large amounts are seen in hairy areas such as the eyebrows, scalp, and upper lip. At delivery the fetal waters are usually muddy with loosened vernix, and the newborn infant looks rather greasy before it has been bathed and carried in again, neat and rosy.

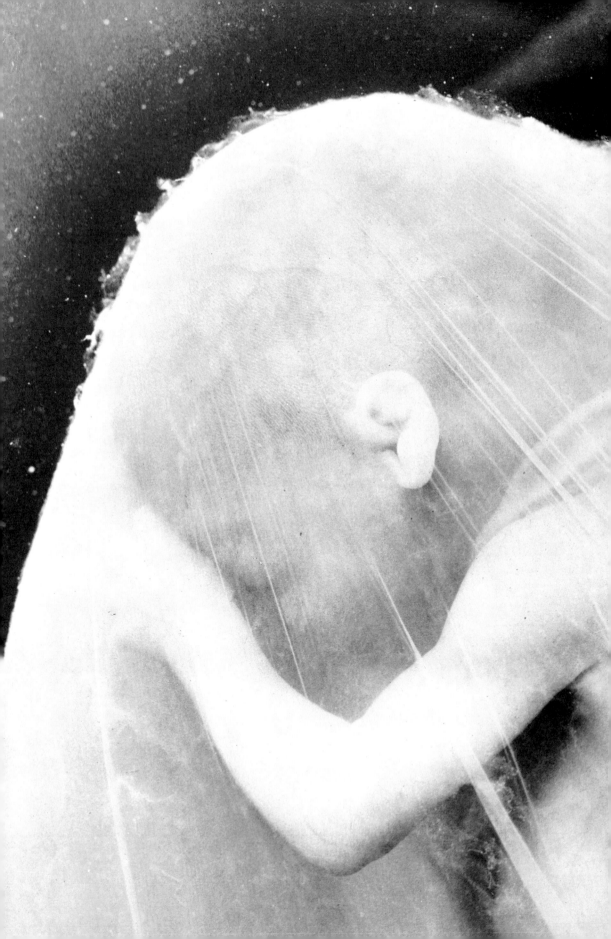

The baby sleeps inside its sheltering envelope. But it is not always asleep while waiting to be born. Rest and quietness alternate with periods of intense activity. The baby exercises its arms and legs with great persistence, bends and stretches its body, sucks, swallows, makes respiratory movements now and then. The space around it is smaller and smaller, so that the baby feels every motion its mother makes. It falls asleep when rocked and wakes up when everything is quiet again, starts at sudden noises but calms down again when its mother and father talk softly to one another. The parents will soon learn what sort of temperament their child has. Some babies are calm and reasonable in the womb, and react only occasionally with a delayed movement of the hand or foot, as though to remind the outside world of their existence. Others are easily upset and protest with vigorous kicks as soon as they are not softly rocked by their mother or if absolute quietness does not prevail. The little being there in the womb is no longer anonymous. It has personality.

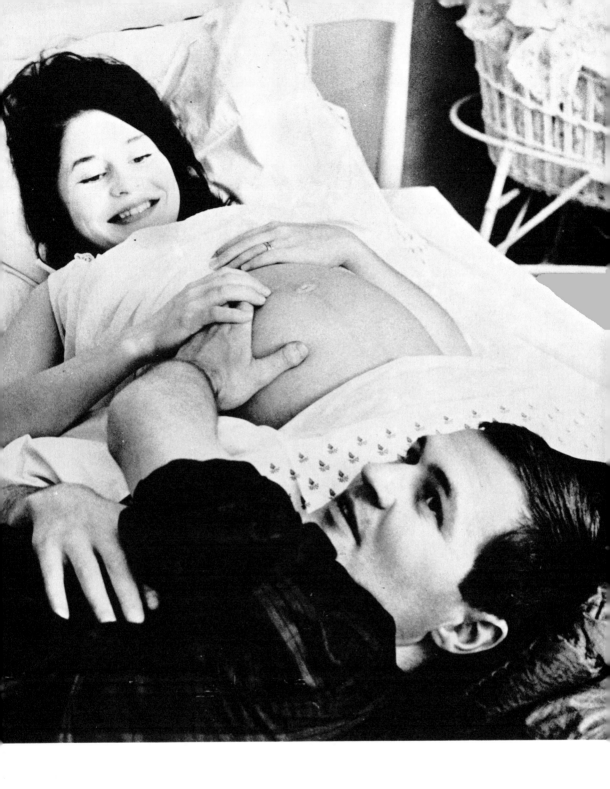

A Third Visit to the Doctor

"Not much time left," the doctor says cheerfully. But the mother-to-be has a good many complaints this time. It is difficult to breathe; she gets out of breath easily; heartburn bothers her; her legs swell; it is difficult to sleep. She is in need of a little sympathy. At home everyone teases her and says that she is expecting quintuplets, and she wonders, naturally, if she is expecting twins.

It is obvious that these physical discomforts are due to the huge space occupied by the womb in the abdominal cavity. The return flow of blood from the legs is somewhat obstructed. This causes swelling in the legs, especially if the mother has been walking or standing to any great extent. This swelling is normal and should not be confused with the swelling that occurs in toxemia.

Position of the fetus

The position of the fetus should be determined. The fetus is so large that it can no longer turn itself spontaneously. On the other hand, it is not so large that the doctor cannot place it in the most favorable position—i.e., with the head down—if it seems to have assumed another position. A head-first delivery is easiest for the mother and least precarious for the baby. If the fetus is upside down (breech presentation) it can sometimes be reversed by means of a so-called external version. The doctor cautiously manipulates the fetus into the right position without having to anesthetize the mother.

At this stage it is often possible to determine whether the birth will be single or multiple. The doctor can tell if the uterus is larger than normal and if it is also wider. If there are twins, the doctor can usually feel at least three large fetal parts: two heads, and one posterior, or vice versa. Also, he can hear fetal heartbeats at two different locations in the uterus, these locations separated by a quiet zone.

Rh factor

During the first examination the expectant mother's blood type has been determined. If her type has proved to be Rh negative, a new blood specimen from the arm is taken to determine if there exists a so-called Rh immunity. This immunity appears in a small number of women in the Rh negative group. When such a woman is pregnant by a man belonging to the Rh positive group, the child will often, but not always, inherit the father's blood type. If later on in pregnancy the placenta is injured, causing the blood corpuscles from the fetus to enter the mother's bloodstream, she will develop antibodies against the fetus's blood. If these antibodies later pass on to the fetus, its own blood corpuscles are destroyed. The baby will then be born with anemia and jaundice, in varying degrees, depending on whether the mother's blood contains few or many antibodies.

In order to save the life of the child, its blood must be exchanged after birth. If on her visits to the doctor before delivery the mother shows antibodies in her blood, the doctor will make preparations for an exchange transfusion in the hospital where the birth will take place. He may choose to induce labor early. Recent dramatic advances in this field have made it possible to diagnose the degree of illness in the unborn child, and even to administer an intra-uterine transfusion. The total antibodies increase with every pregnancy, and the mother's blood must then be tested frequently before full term. But complications of this sort are very rare. There are too many factors which must occur simultaneously for Rh immunity to appear.

Narrow pelvis

By means of several observations the doctor can tell if the pelvis is so narrow that the fetus will have difficulty emerging. For example, if the head is high above the pelvic entrance and can't be pressed down, this can be a sign of a narrow pelvis. With modern X-ray techniques it is possible to determine the exact inner measurement of the pelvis.

Infections

In the late stages of pregnancy the mother should not unnecessarily expose herself to a cold. Even an infection of a relatively light nature can be dangerous if it is present at the time of delivery. This is especially true, as we mentioned, of venereal diseases. Illnesses such as scarlet fever, German measles, or mumps can bring about complications at various stages of pregnancy.

During the last weeks of pregnancy the mother-to-be ought to rest at least one hour in the middle of the day. When she lies down, the blood circulation in the placenta increases, which is to the advantage of the fetus. If the legs are swollen, it is well to lie for a while with the legs raised.

Bleeding

It is important to call the doctor immediately if there is any vaginal bleeding. During the last stages of pregnancy the uterus is very soft and filled with blood. The bleeding could be completely harmless. A strain or pressure, such as that accompanying sexual intercourse, can result in vaginal bleeding. But bleeding can also be a sign of a complication calling for immediate hospitalization. It can be a question of a misplaced placenta *(placenta previa)* or a premature separation of it. When the labor pains begin, there is usually a flow of bloody mucus from the vagina. It is therefore difficult for the mother to decide what the bleeding means.

Nausea and itching

Perhaps the mother has felt nauseous at times. Pregnancy puts a strain on the liver, and therefore pregnant women often feel bilious. In this event it is best to keep to a light diet, avoiding fats and hard-to-digest dishes.

At times a rather irritating itching sensation is felt over the entire body. This is because of a change in the function of the liver, and is difficult to treat. It disappears by itself when the baby arrives, but before that time it can be troublesome. Antihistamines may help.

Labor pains

We do not yet know exactly what sets these in motion. When the neck of the uterus is thinned out, this is a sign that delivery will soon occur. This can be observed by internal examination. If the head places itself in the pelvic entrance and the abdomen falls forward (so-called "lightening") this is a rather good sign, in the case of a woman expecting her first child, that delivery will take place within four weeks. This is not true of women expecting second or subsequent children.

Many women experience so-called preliminary pains long before delivery. The uterus contracts during the entire time of pregnancy, but more noticeably closer to delivery date. If the mother is tired and anemic, these pains can be rather severe. They are different in nature from the real labor pains. When the latter set in, the canal at the mouth of the uterus begins to open. At this point the mucous plug, which has closed off the canal during the months of pregnancy and thus kept out infection, vanishes. The mucus is thick, sticky, and often mixed with blood. When it appears, this is a sure sign that labor has begun in earnest.

If the water breaks before the pains begin it is wise to go to the hospital. The doctor will then examine the position of the fetus to see that its head is properly placed in the pelvic entrance. Otherwise, the woman may be kept in bed, because if the baby's head moves about and is situated high, there is a certain danger that the umbilical cord will become wrapped about it. Because of the additional danger of infection when the membranes rupture, an attempt is often made to induce labor if it does not start normally within a few hours.

What about an anesthetic? Many types are available if mother and doctor feel it necessary. If either laughing gas or trilene is used, it is breathed in just as the pains begin. Sometimes women are delivered under a spinal, regional, or local nerve block. In the great majority of cases, the patient can be given a choice. Occasionally a situation arises in which one form of anesthesia is safer than others. This is one of the many things the mother-to-be and her doctor should discuss before labor begins. Many mothers prefer not to have heavy medication, because they want to be conscious the minute the baby is born and to hear its first cry.

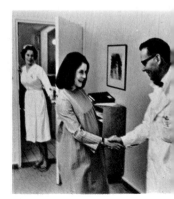

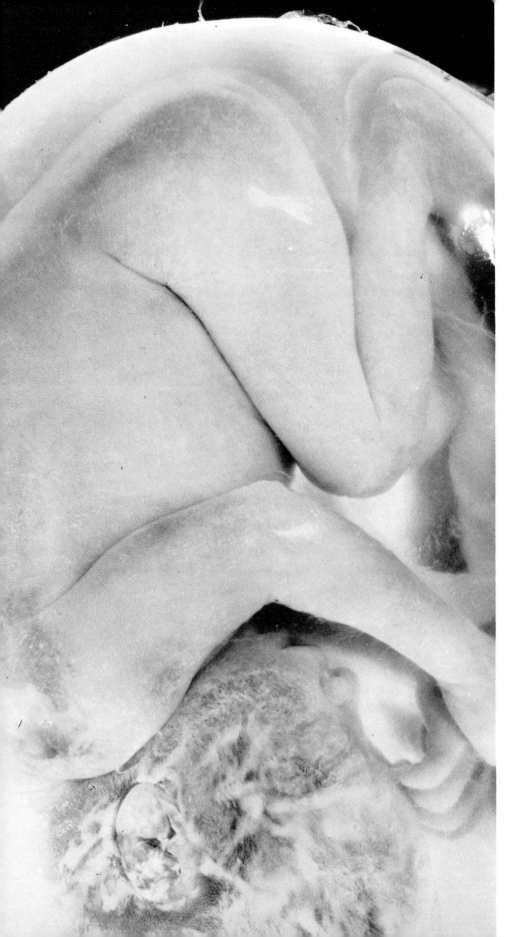

6½ months
13 inches

Waiting

The last months seem very long. Everything is ready now, the baby has only to grow. From the seventh month until term it increases its length from 13 to 20 inches and nearly triples its weight. A thick layer of adipose tissue develops under the skin. This layer serves both as insulation and food supply and confers on the newborn infant its characteristic chubbiness. The finger and toe nails grow, eventually reaching beyond the fingertips. Often the fingernails have to be cut immediately after birth to avoid scratching. The lanugo hairs are shed together with the vernix. The baby swallows part of them together with fetal fluid and they come out on the first diapers. Much of the vernix sticks on the head, and the nurse carefully washes it off so that the little tuft of hair will be clean and shiny when brushed for the first time.

It might seem that the wait is needlessly long. As far as we know it is not the baby who decides the time of delivery, but the placenta and the uterine musculature. Besides, it is to the advantage of the baby to have time to prepare itself for life in the outside world. It is not just a question of survival but of making the first critical adjustments with a favorable margin.

For the mother-to-be these last weeks seem like a sort of limbo. Once the baby's head has slipped down into the pelvic cavity everything is ready for the delivery. There is no use making plans; tomorrow may be the day. Now the expectant mother must live from one day to the next, from hour to hour. Pregnancy is never as long as when it is just about to end. To the woman who must wait it seems infinite, as though she has always been pregnant and will be pregnant forever.

Now delivery is due any day. During the last weeks the womb has been active; now and then it contracts and gets hard, and sometimes causes an ache in the back. It is preparing for the real labor.

Maybe in a few days, maybe tomorrow, she will hold the baby in her arms, look at it, enjoy the clean smell of her newborn infant. How will it look in the blue sweater with the little bonnet? Maybe they won't fit at all. Funny how clearly one imagines the baby; after all, it may not be dark-haired. Will she love it more if it is a girl, or a boy?

This is her last chance to dream of the ideal baby, to think of every little kick as a greeting from the dream child. Now it is a matter of days, maybe only hours, until the breathless moment when dreams are set aside for one little helpless being who from then on is the finest baby in the world.

146

It has been going on the whole morning. First it seemed as though the ordinary contractions had increased their strength. Then pains began to come more regularly, about once every half hour. During the last few hours the intervals have grown shorter and shorter. The first stage of delivery, the dilation stage, has started.

Now the cervical canal, which has been closed during the whole pregnancy, must dilate so that the baby can pass through. The uterus is firmly anchored to the bottom of the pelvis; each contraction will therefore press the upper wall of the uterus down toward the cervix. But the fetal fluid—like all other fluids—is not compressible. It will expand the membranes toward the point of least resistance. A bulging of the membranes will result, pressing down through the cervical canal. The baby's head then follows and dilates it further.

The mother has been told to stay up and move around during the first stage. But now it is getting rather tiring. There are pains every five minutes. Time to set off for the hospital.

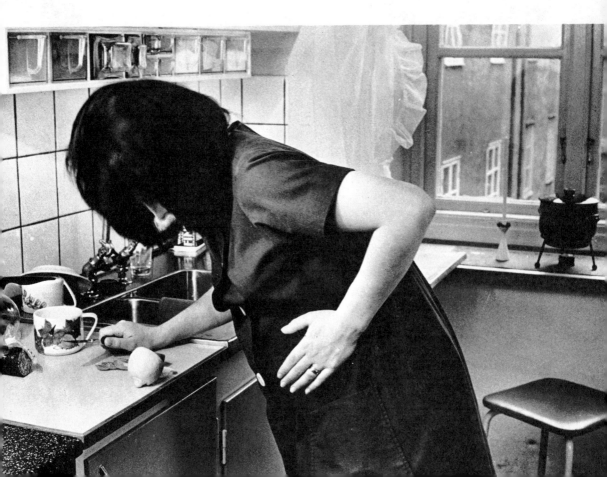

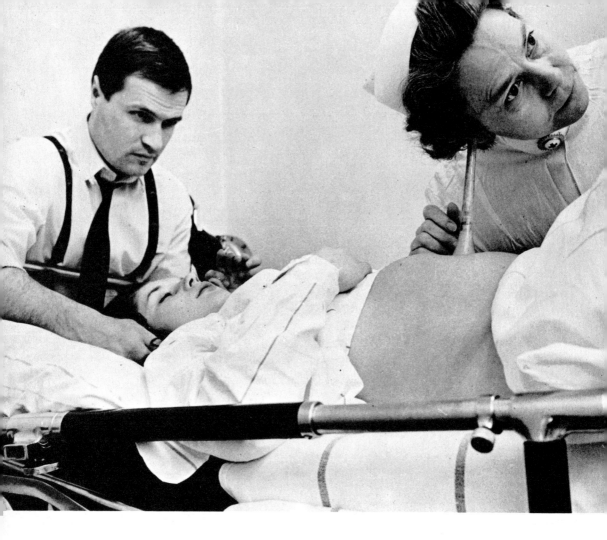

The nurse listens. Yes, the baby is well. At each contraction the muscle fibers of the uterine wall compress the cavity further and the baby will have very little space for a while. But each time there is a pause, fresh blood streams into the placenta, and the baby's heartbeats, which slow down and even become a little irregular during the contractions, resume their normal frequency and are strong and regular again.

The mother rests. She must save her strength until the expulsive stage, when she is both allowed and encouraged to assist. Now there is not much she can do, only relax and try to remember what they told her during the prenatal classes about bending, curving her back, breathing with the whole abdomen, and trying not to strain during the contractions.

The father feels rather awkward, out of place. But he can do much to help his wife—rub her back as the pains grow stronger, cool her face with a nice wet towel when she feels hot and sweaty, console her when things get tedious. Above all, he's the one she wants near her, the one she feels safe with.

The baby's head has come down through the wide-open cervix and stands in the pelvic outlet; one sees it appear at each contraction. In the vaginal opening, more and more of the baby's crown with its black hair is coming into sight.

She feels like pushing out her whole abdomen. "Come on, just a little more—good girl—push harder —now relax, the contraction is over; breathe deeply; let your baby get plenty of air—here you go, push again. . . ."

Now something has to happen. How long can she push and push on that big thing down there? It has to get out, out, out . . .

Delivery

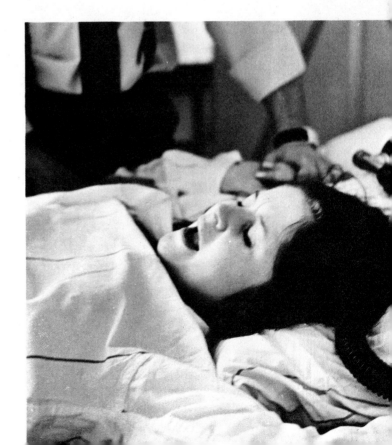

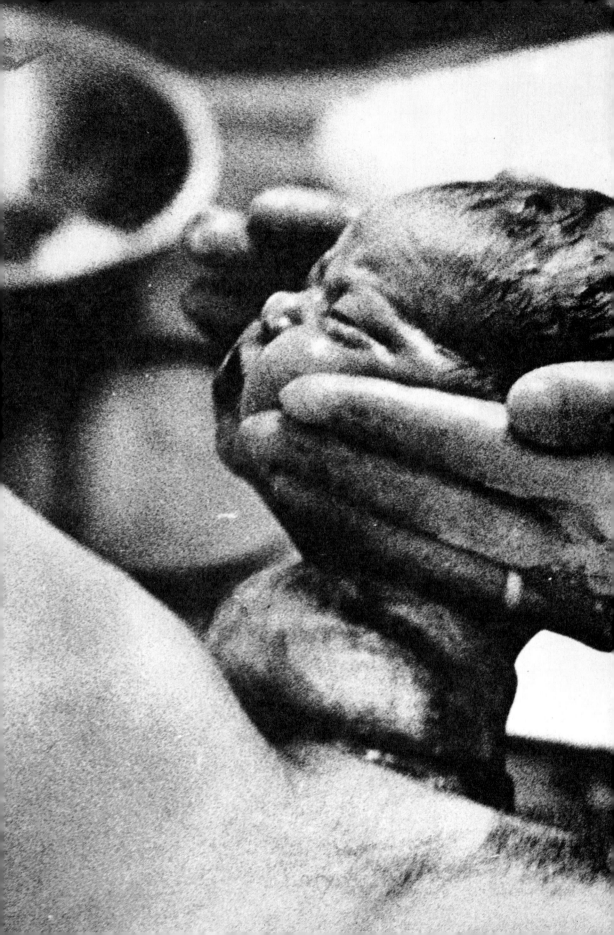

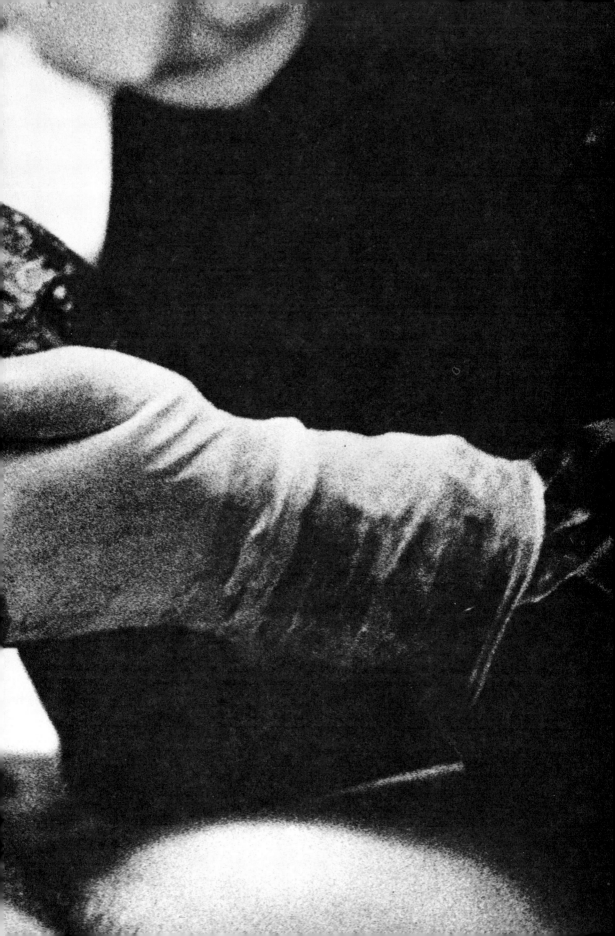

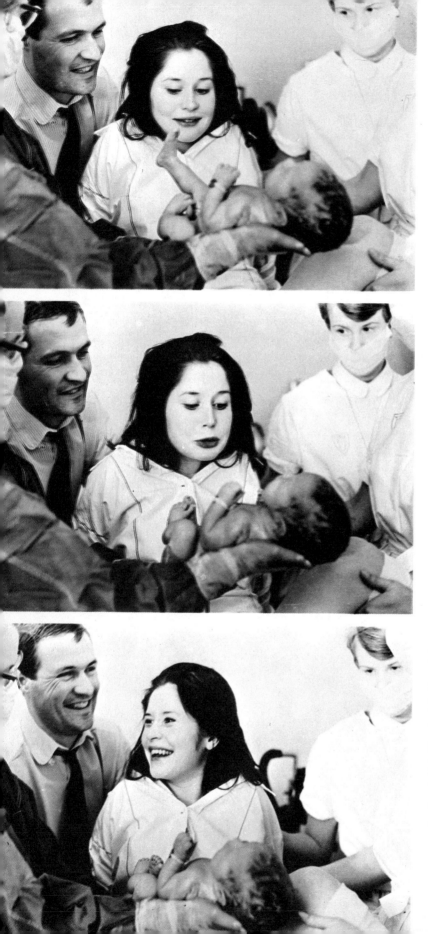

A new little citizen in a big strange world. And now that the blood is no longer pulsating through the cord, because it is now oxygenated in the lungs, filled with air by the first cries, the doctor deftly cuts the tie between mother and child.

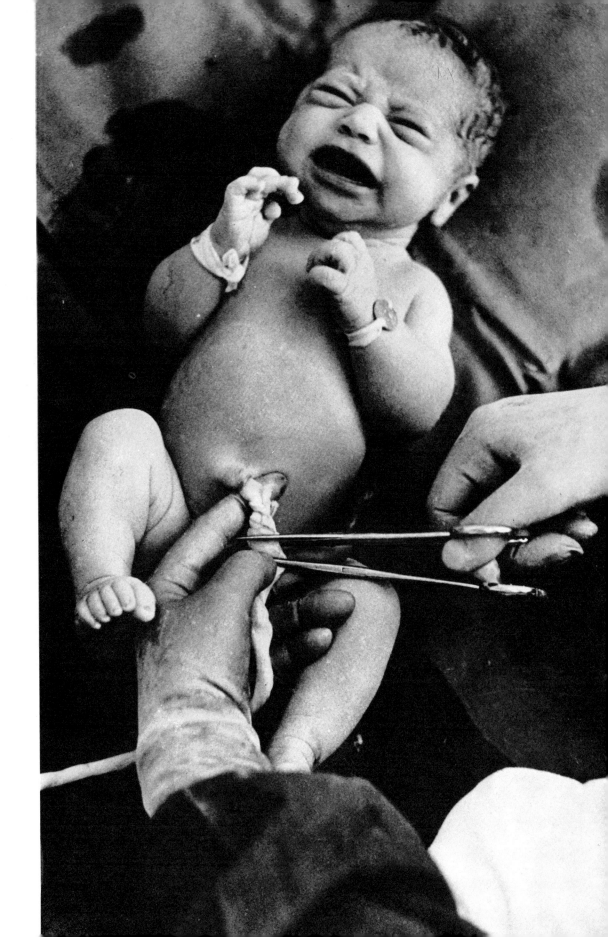

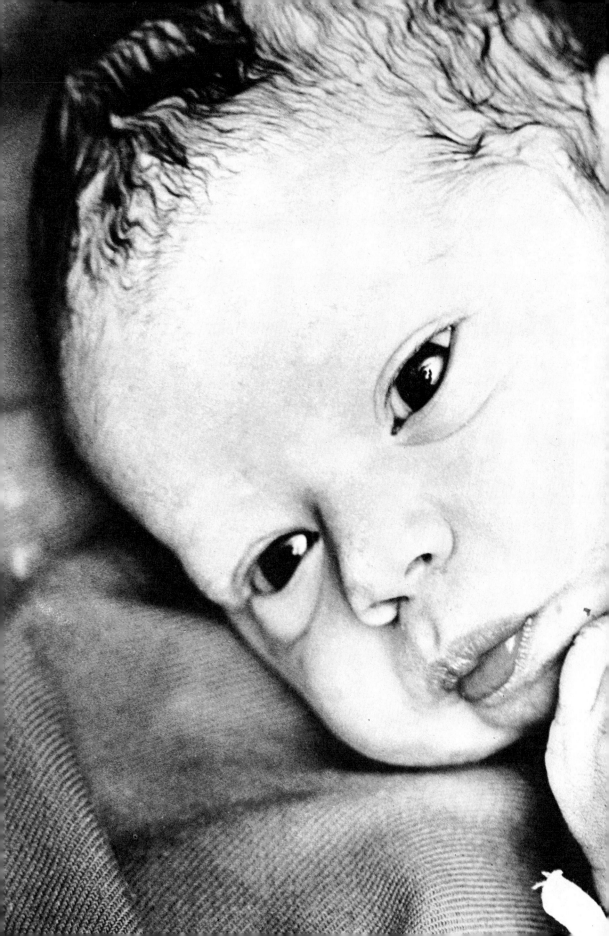

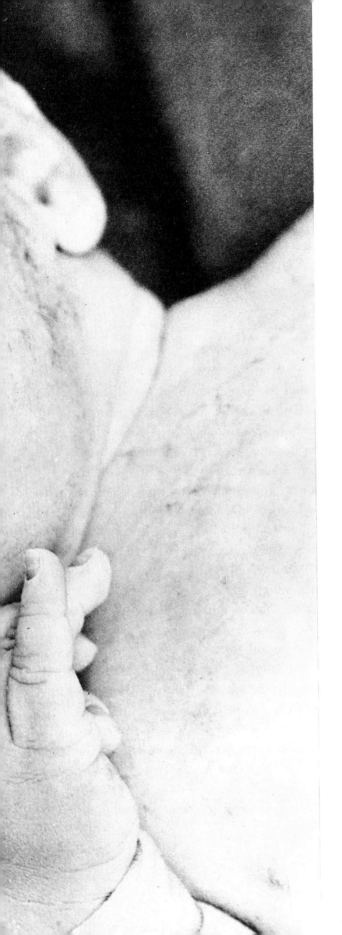

So tiny and defenseless—stark
naked, cannot walk, cannot talk
or ask for anything. He looks at
you with eyes that do not understand what they see. But help-
lessness is power: the newborn
child lies safe, wrapped in its
blanket. Safe because he does
not know of fear, because those
to whom he has come need only
look at him to know that they
would do anything in the
world to protect him.

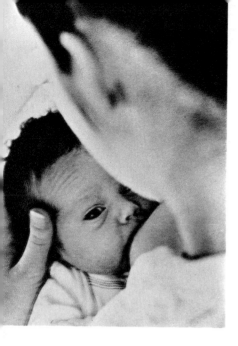

After Birth

It is an immense change to come from the warm closeness of the womb out into a wide world with changes of temperature, to exchange the constant flow of nourishment through the placenta for six meals a day. After floating weightlessly in the fetal waters, it is rather hard to keep one's head upright out in this ocean of air.

The baby gets hungry. This is a new sensation for someone who has never been without food for a single minute. Now he has to work hard for food. The baby fills its lungs with air, cries, and cries some more. Fortunately this is all that is needed. Soon the nourishment from his mother's blood will stream once again into the baby via the warm milk from her breast.

Except for the fact that the baby has difficulty getting around during the first months, he is actually rather well equipped. He has his own way of letting others know when he is dissatisfied or hungry; he can grip and cling; he can suck and swallow. All these things have been practiced for months; none of them needs to be learned all at once when he comes into the world.

Every day his skills increase. The jerky and erratic waving of arms and legs turns into deliberate, controlled motions. The baby will soon follow things with his eyes, and then begin the endless, persevering exercises of trying to look at a thing and grasp it at the same time. It won't be long before he is strong enough to sit nicely upright on his mother's knee.

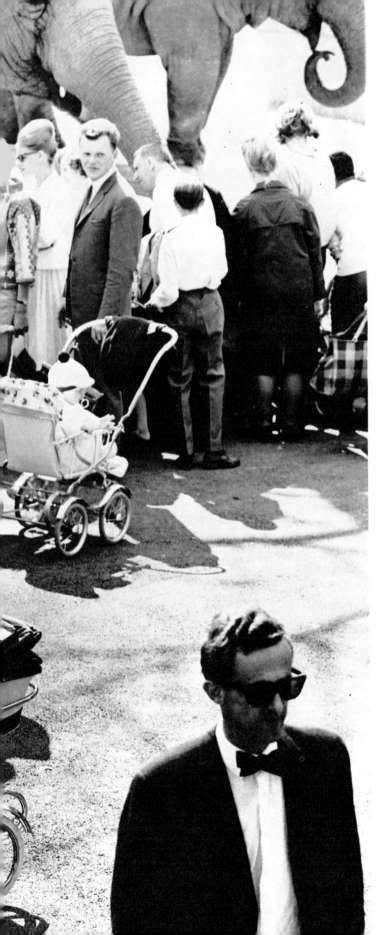

The end of the story? No, only
the beginning. We are born into
the world early, as soon as we
are big enough to survive
outside the womb. But like
all children this child, who
began to exist a year ago, will
need many years of tender care
from loving parents before
he becomes a finished human
being. If we ever are.

INDEX